Primary Sources of World Cultures™

ITALY

A PRIMARY SOURCE CULTURAL GUIDE

Lesli J. Favor, Ph.D.

The Rosen Publishing Group's
PowerPlus Books™
New York

For Joann, in honor of your Italian roots

Published in 2004 by The Rosen Publishing Group, Inc.
29 East 21st Street, New York, NY 10010

First Edition

Library of Congress Cataloging-in-Publication Data

Favor, Lesli J.
Italy : a primary source cultural guide / Lesli J. Favor.
p. cm. — (Primary sources of world cultures)
Includes bibliographical references and index.
ISBN 0-8239-3839-5 (library binding)
1. Italy—Juvenile literature.
I. Title. II. Series.
DG417 .F38 2003
945—dc21

2002015435

Manufactured in the United States of America

Cover images: A golden sculpture of a woman rests on the bow of a gondola *(foreground)* in the Regata Storica in Venice. A folio *(background)* from Codex Leicester by Leonardo da Vinci.

Photo Credits: Cover (background) © Seth Joel/Corbis; cover (middle) © Mark L. Stephenson; pp. 3, 120, 122 © 2002 GeoAtlas; pp. 4 (top), 15 © Sandro Vannini/Corbis; pp. 4 (middle and bottom), 52, 53 © The Image Works; pp. 5 (top), 41 (top), 91 © Stephanie Maze/Corbis; pp. 5 (middle), 55 © John Slater/Corbis; pp. 5 (bottom), 16, 110 © Vittoriano Rastelli/Corbis; p. 6 © Ric Ergenbright/Corbis; p. 7 © Morton Beebe/Corbis; pp. 8, 72, 77, 120 (middle inset) © Dallas and John Heaton/Corbis; p. 9 © Granata Press/The Image Works; p. 10 © Roberto Arakaki/International Stock; p. 11 © Lance Nelson/Corbis; p. 12 © Dennis Marsico/Corbis; pp. 13, 17, 95 © Mike Yamashata/Woodfin Camp & Associates; pp. 14, 121 © Matton Images; p. 18 © Wesley Bocxe/Photo Researchers, Inc.; p. 19 © Karl Weatherly/Corbis; p. 20 © Art Resource; pp. 21, 50, 62 © Archivo Iconografico, S.A./Corbis; pp. 22 (top), 66 © Elio Ciol/Corbis; pp. 22 (bottom), 86 © Mansell/TimePix; pp. 23, 28 (bottom), 29 (top), 30, 33 (top), 82, 83, 84, 88 © Mary Evans Picture Library; pp. 24, 58 © Archive/Photo Researchers, Inc.; p. 25 © Lauros/Giraudon/Bridgeman Art Library; pp. 26, 71 © Ruggero Vanni/Corbis; p. 27 Courtesy of the General Libraries, The University of Texas, at Austin; p. 28 (top) © Alinari/Art Resource; pp. 29 (bottom), 119 © Francis G. Mayer/Corbis; pp. 31, 32 © Brown Brothers; p. 33 (bottom) © Peter Stackpole/TimePix; p. 34 © Thomas D. McAvoy/TimePix; p. 35 © Archivo storico della camera del deputati and Biblioteca della camera del deputati; pp. 36, 89, 113, 116 © AP/Wide World Photos; pp. 37, 57, 99, 100 © Owen Franken/Corbis; pp. 38, 42 © The Pierpont Morgan Library/Art Resource; pp. 39, 80 © Bridgeman Art Library; pp. 43, 51, 81 © AKG London; pp. 44, 47 © Reunion des Musees Nationaux/Art Resource; p. 45 © Werner Forman Archive; p. 48 © Gilles Mermet/Art Resource; pp. 54, 103 © Reuters NewMedia Inc./Corbis; p. 56 © AFP/Corbis; pp. 59, 63 © Scala/Art Resource; p. 60 © Alessandro Bianchi/AFP Photo; p. 61 © Tibor Bognar/Corbis; p. 64 © M. Bertinetti/Photo Researchers, Inc.; p. 65 © Michael St. Maur Sheil/Corbis; p. 67 © Edimedia/Corbis; p. 68 © Gianni Tortoli/Photo Researchers, Inc.; pp. 69, 106 © Hulton Archive/Getty Images; p. 70 © Alinari/Art Resource; pp. 73, 120 (left inset) © Jon Davison/Lonely Planet Images; p. 74 © Roger Antrobus/Corbis; pp. 75 (top), 105 © Gianni Dagli Orti/Corbis; p. 75 (bottom) © Araldo de Luca/Corbis; pp. 76, 104 © Ted Spiegel/Corbis; pp. 78, 120 (right inset) © Bettmann/Corbis; p. 79 © Christie's Images; p. 85 © Giunti Gruppo Editoriale, Firenze/Archives Charmet/Private Collection/Bridgeman Art Library; pp. 87, 112 © Photofest; p. 90 © Paul Almasy/Corbis; p. 92 (top) © M. Courtney-Clarke/Photo Researchers, Inc.; p. 92 (bottom) © Michael S. Yamashita/Corbis; pp. 93, 94 © Lesli Favor; p. 96 © Chris Selby/Image State/Pictor; p. 97 © Gary Braasch/Woodfin Camp & Associates; p. 98 (top) © Brent Winebrenner/Photri, Inc.; p. 98 (bottom) © Hubert Stadler/Corbis; p. 101 © Action Images/Icon Sports Media; p. 102 © GrantPix/Photo Researchers, Inc.; p. 107 © Jonathan Blair/Corbis; p. 108 © David Lees/Corbis; p. 111 (top) © John Heseltine/Corbis; p. 111 (bottom) © David Lees/TimePix.

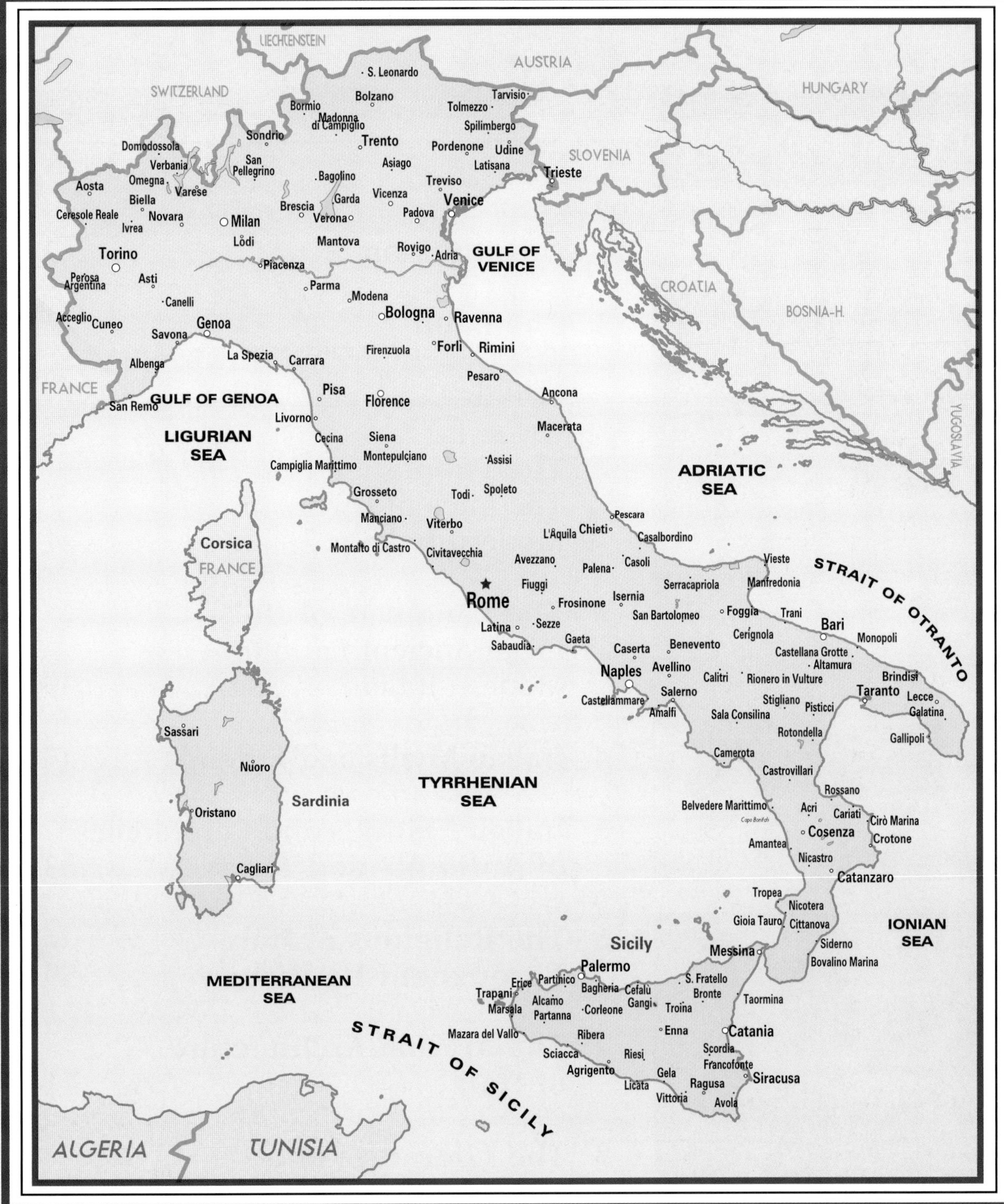
LIECHTENSTEIN
AUSTRIA
SWITZERLAND
HUNGARY
S. Leonardo
Bolzano
Tarvisio
Bormio
Madonna di Campiglio
Tolmezzo
Spilimbergo
Sondrio
Trento
Pordenone
Udine
Domodossola
San Pellegrino
Asiago
Latisana
SLOVENIA
Verbania
Omegna
Bagolino
Treviso
Trieste
Aosta
Varese
Garda
Vicenza
Biella
Brescia
Venice
Ceresole Reale
Novara
Verona
Padova
Ivrea
Milan
Lodi
Mantova
Rovigo
Adria
GULF OF VENICE
Torino
Piacenza
Perosa Argentina
Asti
Parma
CROATIA
Modena
Canelli
Bologna
Ravenna
BOSNIA-H.
Acceglio
Cuneo
Genoa
Savona
Forli
Rimini
Firenzuola
La Spezia
Carrara
Albenga
Pesaro
FRANCE
Pisa
Ancona
San Remo
GULF OF GENOA
Florence
Livorno
YUGOSLAVIA
LIGURIAN SEA
Cecina
Siena
Macerata
Montepulciano
Assisi
Campiglia Marittimo
ADRIATIC SEA
Grosseto
Todi
Spoleto
Manciano
Viterbo
Pescara
Corsica
FRANCE
L'Aquila
Chieti
Casalbordino
Montalto di Castro
Civitavecchia
Avezzano
Palena
Casoli
Vieste
STRAIT OF OTRANTO
Fiuggi
Serracapriola
Manfredonia
Rome
Frosinone
Isernia
Foggia
San Bartolomeo
Trani
Latina
Sezze
Bari
Cerignola
Monopoli
Sabaudia
Gaeta
Caserta
Benevento
Castellana Grotte
Altamura
Naples
Avellino
Calitri
Rionero in Vulture
Brindisi
Taranto
Castellammare
Salerno
Stigliano
Lecce
Amalfi
Pisticci
Sala Consilina
Galatina
Sassari
Rotondella
Gallipoli
Camerota
Nuoro
Castrovillari
TYRRHENIAN SEA
Rossano
Sardinia
Belvedere Marittimo
Acri
Cariati
Oristano
Cirò Marina
Cosenza
Crotone
Amantea
Nicastro
Cagliari
Catanzaro
Tropea
Nicotera
Gioia Tauro
Cittanova
IONIAN SEA
Sicily
Siderno
Messina
Bovalino Marina
Palermo
MEDITERRANEAN SEA
Erice
Partinico
S. Fratello
Trapani
Bagheria
Cefalù
Bronte
Alcamo
Gangi
Marsala
Partanna
Corleone
Troina
Taormina
Mazara del Vallo
Ribera
Enna
Catania
STRAIT OF SICILY
Sciacca
Riesi
Scordia
Agrigento
Francofonte
Gela
Siracusa
Licata
Ragusa
Vittoria
Avola
ALGERIA
TUNISIA

CONTENTS

INTRODUCTION

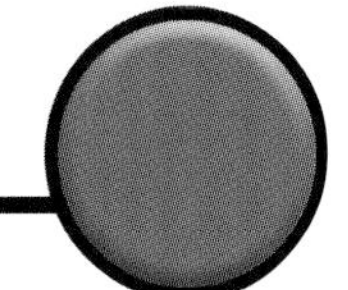

There is a well-known story about Italian history. The year was 1870, and for the first time since the fall of the Roman Empire, all of Italy was united as one kingdom. The first king, Victor Emmanuel II, arrived by carriage in Rome. This city was the jewel in his crown, the capital of the kingdom. He exclaimed, "Well, we've finally made it!" The king spoke in the dialect of Piedmonte, for there was not yet a national language. Another Piedmontese politician, Massimo d'Azeglio, in the united kingdom summed up the real state of affairs: "We have made Italy; now we must make Italians."

One way or another, the making of Italians had been continuous since around 4000 BC. Archaeological finds show that Paleolithic nomadic hunter-gatherers roamed across Italy as many as 70,000 years ago.

By approximately 1800 BC, Italy had been settled by about a dozen tribes, including the Umbrians, the Veneti, and the Sicles. From these tribes, some of the regions of modern Italy gained their names: Umbria, Veneto, Sicily, and so on. The seeds of Italian identity had taken root. Despite the 3,000 or so years separating these early peoples from the founders of the kingdom of Italy in 1861, they all helped to create Italian culture and the country of Italy as it is known today.

People walk among pigeons at Piazza San Marco *(left)* in Venice, Italy. Saint Mark's Square, once called the "drawing room of the world" by French playwright Alfred de Musset, has been the scene for much of Venice's religious, political, and social life for more than a millennium. Statues of Venice's patron saints, Saint Marco and Saint Todaro, peer down from the top of the Byzantine-style St. Mark's Basilica, which houses the remains of Saint Marco the Evangelist beneath its altar. This ancient Roman road *(above)*, the Ostian Way, in Ostia, is the site where Saint Paul's remains were deposited. Ostia is a small, quiet town located north of Rome between the Tiber River and the Tyrrhenian Sea.

The Spanish Steps, or Scalinata di Spagna, located at the Piazza di Spagna in Rome, were designed by an Italian and paid for by the French in 1725 to lead to the French church Trinità dei Monti. However, the steps derived their name from the Spanish Embassy that is still present on the piazza. As far back as the eighteenth century, Italy's most beautiful men and women have gathered on the steps, waiting to be chosen as an artist's model. Today, the steps remain a popular tourist attraction.

Even now in the twenty-first century, Italy bears clear evidence of the defining qualities of its past. Ancient Etruscan ruins and burial sites are a valuable reminder of the pre-Roman era. Remains of the Romans themselves are ever evident, for their roads, walls, aqueducts, and amphitheaters continue to stand as symbols of the empire's glory days. From the Renaissance period, glorious artworks and music add grace and beauty to the Italian identity. The Roman Catholic Church, whose followers in Italy date to the first century AD, reigns from its tiny nation within Italy, Vatican City. Every year, millions of tourists travel from around the world to enrich their senses with Italian art and culture and to see the beauty of the land itself.

Exclusive shops line Via Montenapoleone, the most elegant shopping street in Milan. Italians have succeeded in industrializing the manufacture of high-quality ready-to-wear designer clothes. Italian fashion is a leader among the country's exports, boasting higher figures than both cars and chemicals. Milan's fashion fairs often attract more attention than the catwalks of Paris or New York. Milan is also home to the world's most important publishing houses and the largest television companies.

While so much about Italy and the Italians seems ancient, modern Italy is situated firmly in the present. Like other industrialized nations, Italy has problems of joblessness, illegal immigration, political conflicts, national debt, and crime. But true to its past, the country has taken a progressive stance in the global forum. Italy was a founding member of the European Union (EU). A member of the United Nations since 1955, Italy is also a supporter of the North Atlantic Treaty Organization (NATO), the General Agreement on Tariffs and Trade/World Trade Organization, and other similar measures. In 2003, Italy will serve as president of the EU for six months, the general period served by its partnering nations.

The process of creating the Italian identity is ongoing. The latest symbol of change is Italy's monetary unit. The coins of the Roman Empire, of course, are long gone. For more than 1,000 years, the lira, introduced in Europe by Charlemagne (c. 742–814), was Italy's currency. More recently, in January 2002, the euro replaced the lira, uniting Italy's currency with that of Europe.

THE LAND

The Geography and Environment of Italy

Italy extends into the Mediterranean Sea from southern Europe. Its landmass is made up of a boot-shaped peninsula, the large islands of Sicily and Sardinia, and numerous smaller islands. With a total land area of 113,521 square miles (294,020 square kilometers), Italy is the fourth largest country in western Europe, smaller in size only to France, Spain, and Germany. It is bordered in the north by Switzerland and Austria, in the northwest by France, and in the northeast by Slovenia.

The Geography of Italy

Most of Italy's terrain is rugged and mountainous, with some plains and coastal lowlands. Dominating the mainland are two mountain ranges that march across the top and along the center of the boot. Along the northern border are the Alps, extending from France in the west to Slovenia and beyond in the east. Stretching like a spine, the Apennines range dominates the Italian coastline. Plunging nearly to the sea, these jagged mountains leave little room for flat coasts and sandy beaches. Its highest peak is the Corno Grande, 9,560 feet (2,914 meters) high. These mountains are composed almost entirely of marble, which has been mined since ancient Roman times.

The Dolomites *(left)* are the range of eastern Alps located in northeastern Italy. These dolomitic limestone peaks, which rise to a height of 10,965 feet (3,344 meters), are famous for their vivid coloring at sunrise and sunset. Many national parks dot this region along with quaint towns and storybook castles. Taormina *(above)*, a small medieval city in Sicily, is one of the island's most popular resorts. The city is situated on a plateau below Mount Tauro. From this location it is possible to view the splendor of Sicily and one of Europe's greatest natural wonders, Mount Etna.

Italy's coastline covers 75 percent of its land borders, which curve into inlets and coves, totaling 4,712 miles (7,600 kilometers). The major southern port city of Naples is located on the southwest coast. Other important port cities are Trieste, Venice, Bari, Genoa, Palermo on the island of Sicily, and Porto Torres in Sardinia.

The waters of the Mediterranean—a large sea that lies between Europe and Africa—continuously wash the shores of Italy and its islands. The Mediterranean is made up of many smaller seas. To the west of the boot's top, and along the south of France, lies the Ligurian Sea. The part of the Mediterranean washing Italy's western shore is the Tyrrhenian Sea. The Adriatic Sea lies along Italy's eastern coast. Farther south, the Ionian Sea touches the lower shores of the peninsula and eastern Sicily. The Gulf of Taranto creates a natural southern harbor.

Rivers and Lakes

In northern Italy, between the Alps and the Apennines, lies the country's only large area of flat and fertile land known as the Po River Valley. Flowing through it is the Po, Italy's longest river, whose earliest name, Bodincus, meant "bottomless." Fed by more than 100 tributaries carrying fresh water from the mountains, the 405-mile (652-kilometer) long waterway empties into the Adriatic Sea. On the banks of the Po, in the Piedmonte region, lies Turin, Italy's fourth-largest city.

Italy's second-longest river is the Adige, a 254-mile (406-kilometer) waterway that flows through Verona and empties into the Adriatic Sea just south of Venice. Other major rivers are the Volturno in Campania, which empties into the Tyrrhenian, and the Arno, which flows through Florence and Pisa and empties into the Ligurian Sea.

The field and farmhouse pictured here are located in the Po River Valley, nourished by the Po River. The great river is fed by 141 tributaries and winds along a plain that stretches across northern Italy from France to the Adriatic Sea. Towns along the Po are home to a wealth of art, as well as quintessential Italian food.

Italy's historic city of Florence was built on the site of an Etruscan settlement. Once a splendid Renaissance city, Florence was originally a small, rural town, but because of its artistic importance, it became an important city that set creative standards for many cities throughout Europe. Florence's cultural and economic wealth flourished under the Medici family in the fifteenth and sixteenth centuries. Six hundred years of extraordinary artistic achievement can be seen in its thirteenth-century cathedral, the Ponte Vecchio Bridge, the Santa Croce Church, and the Uffizi Palace.

The Tiber, yet another large river, makes its way past the historic city of Rome on its way to the Tyrrhenian Sea. Just 15 miles (24 kilometers) inland, Rome—Italy's capital city—sprawls atop the famous seven hills (Palatine, Capitoline, Caelian, Esquitine, Aventine, Quirinal, and Viminal) and controls a key river crossing that includes a midstream island.

Italy has about 1,500 lakes, many of them small Alpine lakes formed by glaciers, the largest of which are in valleys of the Alpine foothills. These lakes include Garda, Maggiore, Como, Iseo, and Lugano. In Latium, lakes such as Bolsena and Albano fill the craters of extinct volcanoes. Lesina and Varano are coastal lakes in Puglia.

Mountains

Along Italy's northern border, the Alps tower majestically, shielding Italy's lake district and reaching as high as 12,480 feet

The Apennine Mountains divide Italy, splitting the country into east and west zones. Along this mountain range occurs the highest seismic activity in the country. The Irpinia earthquake, with a magnitude of 6.9, happened in the Apennine Mountain region and was one of Italy's most severe geological events in recent history.

(3,840 meters). The peaks jut upward in scenic formations, some of their highest points lying between Italy and its bordering countries. One such Alpine peak is called Monte Bianco, which lies along the Italian-French border, and another, Monte Rosa, which lies along the Italian-Swiss border. In fact, the Alps contain some of the highest European peaks, as well as Italy's highest peak of all. Long ago, glaciers flowed through the valleys of the Alps, gouging the landscape as they passed. Today, a least a thousand glaciers remain, although they are slowly vanishing. Since 1950, more than a hundred glaciers have disappeared.

Travel between Italy and its bordering countries takes place through Alpine passes, just as it did during ancient times. Today, however, highways and railroads carry travelers through the mountains more quickly. In the northwestern section of the Alps, travelers enter France through the Little Saint Bernard Pass, and enter Switzerland through the Great Saint Bernard Pass.

Farther east is the Passo Del San Gottardo, or Saint Gotthard Pass. Leading into Switzerland, it is an important travel route between Italy and the rest of Europe. A highway stretches across the pass, and beneath it lies the St. Gotthard Tunnel. Inside the tunnel is a railroad that carries travelers on a twisted path. The St. Gotthard Road Tunnel, especially for vehicles, was opened in 1980.

Near the eastern end of the Italian Alps, in the section known as the Dolomites, is Brenner Pass, which was favored by the Romans. Connecting Italy and Austria, this pass pushes between breathtaking peaks, many of which tower higher than 10,000 feet (3,000 meters).

Along the backbone of Italy's peninsula stretch the Apennine Mountains, a chain that nearly divides the country in half lengthwise. This 1,235-mile (1,992-kilometer)

Modern houses in Ercolano surround this excavation site of the ancient city of Herculaneum. More than 2,000 years ago, Herculaneum was a seaside resort with approximately five thousand inhabitants until the eruption of Mount Vesuvius in AD 79, which buried the city under 75 feet (23 meters) of ash. For years archaeologists believed the Romans had escaped the wrath of Vesuvius, but in 1984, many carbonized bodies were discovered.

range twists like a snake, nearly spreading to the coast in several places. Its highest peak, known as Corno Grande, lies east of Rome.

Environmental Hazards

Because of its geography, Italy is prone to natural disasters such as floods, volcanic eruptions, and earthquakes. These natural hazards vary depending on the region and its particular climate. For example, the city of Venice, formed of 118 small islands, is slowly sinking into the sea. Many old Venetian buildings are flooded on the ground floors, as they are now below sea level. In addition, the waters of the Adriatic Sea flood Venice as often as ten times a year. Flooding of another sort occurs in the Po River Valley, caused by the river itself. In the past century, some of the worst floods occurred in the autumns of 1951, 1957, and 1966. Hazards in other regions include mudflows, landslides, and avalanches.

Italy has six active volcanoes, all located in the southern Apennines. Besides Greece's volcanic activity, these are the only active volcanoes in Europe. Perhaps the most famous of Italy's volcanoes is Mount Vesuvius, located near Naples. During Roman times, the cities of Pompeii and Herculaneum thrived within sight of Mount Vesuvius. In AD 79, Mount Vesuvius erupted. Hot lava, rocks, and ash descended upon the cities below. The disaster occurred so suddenly that most people were buried by

Italian olives are harvested in November for oil. Workers lay nets around the tree's base to catch the fruits as they fall. Olive trees normally take five years to bear any fruit, but the best olive oil comes from trees that are one to two hundred years old.

lava, hot ash, or falling structures while in the midst of daily activities. The site of the ruins was discovered accidentally in 1713, and excavation of the buried cities began in 1748. Since then, archaeologists have learned a great deal about daily Roman life. Mount Vesuvius has continued to erupt periodically throughout the centuries.

Italy's other active volcanoes include Stromboli and Vulcano (on the Aeolian Islands), the Campi Flegrei and the Island of Ischia (near Naples), and Etna, which is located in Sicily. The volcano Stromboli sends a continuous flow of lava into the sea, although it has not erupted violently since 1921. Also in the Aeolians are vents in the earth's crust known as fumaroles, from which vapors escape.

Flora and Fauna

Italy has three main regions of indigenous vegetation: the Alps, the Po River Valley, and the Mediterranean-Apennine region. At the foot of the Alps, various types of trees dot the landscape. Tall, thin cypress and European olive trees share the land with cork oaks and cherry laurels. Beech, larch, and Norway spruce thrive at a slightly higher elevation, while smaller shrubs such as rhododendron, the dwarf juniper, and the green alder hug the ground at higher elevations. Still higher lie grassy pasturelands with grazing cattle and sheep, and wildflowers such as primrose and rock jasmine. The highest level of vegetation in the Alps, along the snow line, consists of hardy mosses, lichens, and a few plants such as saxifrage.

The wide, flat plain of the Po River Valley boasted forests long ago. But today, few of those trees remain. Most of the vegetation in this region was planted more recently to replenish the environment. Poplars now grow there, and sedges grow in its drier, rockier soil. Where the ground contains a higher concentration of clay, heather and Scotch pines flourish. Along streams and in bogs, grasses carpet the ground, while water lilies grow near marshes. The fertile ground of the Po River Valley also supports edible crops, including corn, wheat, potatoes, and rice.

In the Apennines, pasturelands like those found near the Alps are common. In the lower foothills there are olives, oleanders, carobs, mastics, and Aleppo pines. Sea grapes grow on the dunes along the coast. In southern Italy, traces of the ancient forests of truffle oak, white poplar, and Oriental plane still survive. In Calabria and Puglia, on Italy's southernmost peninsula, there are plentiful beech woods. The island of Sicily is home to papyrus, a freshwater plant, once dried and used as writing paper during ancient times. On Sardinia, feather grasses and other hardy plants grow where the terrain was long ago covered by olive groves.

Very few of Italy's original wildlife species remain. Over the centuries as farms, villages, and

The farmhouses and rolling fields of Pienza are located in the Tuscany region of Italy. Tuscany's lush landscape has been cultivated for centuries. Inhabitants of this area have always exercised great care when farming the land to make it productive while not sacrificing its beauty. Many of Tuscany's farmhouses have been passed down through the generations since the 1500s.

Mouflons, also called the Sardinian wild sheep, are located on the island of Sardinia. Like most wild sheep do, mouflons live in mountainous terrain, usually above the tree line. They are known for their red-brown coloring and a distinctive white circle around the eyes. Both males and females have horns, although the males' horns are normally larger. Over the last fifty years, the mouflon population has decreased due to the loss of habitat, hunting, and interbreeding with domestic sheep.

cities developed, wild animals were aggressively hunted or pushed away. In time, overhunting, combined with destruction of natural habitats, caused a scarcity of wildlife. Animals, particularly large ones, gradually disappeared from Italy's landscape.

Today, a few kinds of wild animals survive. In northern Italy, the Alps are home to ibex (a species of wild goat), chamois (a type of antelope), and roe deer. More rare are lynx and brown bears. Smaller animals include marmots, ermines, and Alpine rabbits. Reptiles include viper snakes. Alpine bird life includes mountain partridges, black grouse, and golden eagles.

Italy's other mountains have wildlife similar to that found in the Alps. In addition, small numbers of wolves and foxes roam the mountains. In Sardinia's mountains, wild boars, fallow deer, and mouflon (wild mountain sheep) prosper. Bird life includes falcons and swallows, and freshwater fish include brown trout, sturgeon, and eel.

The seas on Italy's coasts are home to sponges and coral as well as sharks, tuna, octopuses, swordfish, red mullet, sardines, and anchovies. In damp, dark caves along the coast roost horseshoe bats.

Climate

For the most part, Italy's climate is generally mild with colder northern winters. Weather varies by region, depending on proximity to mountainous areas or the sea.

Courmayeur, located on the Italian side of Monte Bianco, is an internationally renowned area for skiing. Courmayeur is situated at the mouth of the d'Aosta Valley and has more castles and Roman ruins than all of Italy.

The high regions of the Alps are coldest, with long winters and short, cool summers. Below, along the Po River, seasons are more balanced, with snowy winters, rainy springs and autumns, and hot summers. Along the Apennines, winters are cold. Rain is also frequent along the western coast and in the mountains.

Italy's southern coast enjoys warm, dry weather. Sometimes a hot, dry wind, called a sirocco, blows from the south, carrying sand from Africa's Sahara Desert. While Italian art draws millions of tourists to the country each year, part of Italy's attraction belongs to its land and climate. From snowy mountain peaks to sun-baked beaches, Italy is a country of rich diversity.

THE PEOPLE

The Ancient Etruscans and Modern Italians

The people of Italy have a vast cultural heritage with roots in ancient times. While the country's earliest settlers left few traces of its past, the Etruscan culture is considered the first long-standing civilization to develop in central Italy. Later, around 800 BC, Phoenicians settled the island of Sardinia. A couple of hundred years later, Celts settled Milan. During the eighth and seventh centuries BC, Greeks settled in what is now southern Italy. Around 600 BC, they established Naples, a major port city in modern Italy's region of Campania, on the Tyrrhenian Sea. To the north of the Greeks, Romans and other groups settled, eventually overtaking Etruscan territory.

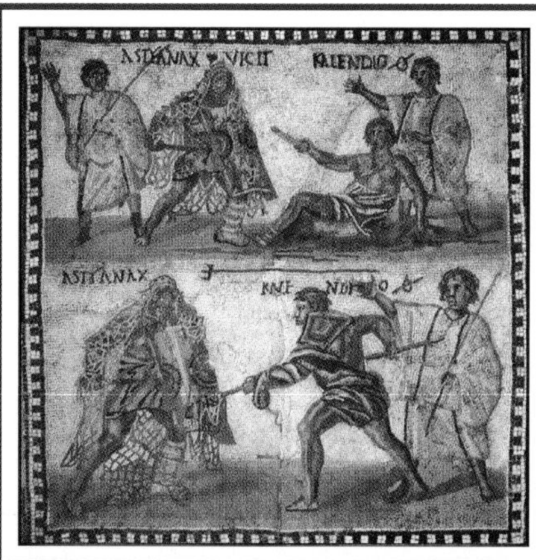

The Etruscans

Some historians believe that various groups of people—known now as the Etruscans—migrated from Asia Minor to Tuscany at the end of the twelfth century BC. "Tuscany" means "the land of the Etruscans." The Romans called these people the *Etrusci* or *Tusci*. From the seventh to the sixth centuries BC, Etruscan culture was at its height. Skilled engineers who built roads and mines, knowledgeable farmers, and talented artisans all contributed to the development of the community. Much of what we know about the Etruscans comes from archaeological remains and artifacts found in tombs and religious sanctuaries. (Because they

The sixth-century sarcophagus of a married couple on a funeral bed *(left)* is considered a common method of burial for the period. It was discovered in the Etruscan city of Cerveteri. This fourth-century mosaic illustration *(above)* depicts gladiator fights, common public entertainment in ancient Rome. Two opponents usually fought until one died or was left unarmed. Many gladiators used nicknames to conceal their low status in society as slaves, captives, and prisoners of war. However, inside the Colosseum, these men focused public attention on the ultimate Roman ideals of courage, stoicism, and bravery.

This Etruscan gold coin exemplifies the metalwork unrivaled in the Mediterranean during the first millennium BC. Scholars believe that Etruscan metalworking remains unmatched in quality even by contemporary standards. Etruscans prided themselves on the technique of filigree, the crafting of delicate gold wire requiring enormous effort and time. Even today, modern historians wonder how they did it, especially given their primitive tools.

believed in the afterlife, many Etruscans were buried with pottery, clothing, ornaments, and weapons.) Their painted tombs, depicting scenes of everyday life, provide important information about how these ancient people lived.

The first Etruscan towns were built near the coast of the Tyrrhenian Sea, which gets its name from *Tyrrhenoi*, the Greek name for the Etruscans. Later, the Etruscans spread inland, building twelve main cities, many of which were surrounded by walls that offered protection to the inhabitants. Well-constructed roads crossed the enclosed cities, while drainage and sewage systems carried away waste. Volterra, with a population of nearly 100,000 people, had approximately ten miles (sixteen kilometers) of city walls. By the sixth century BC, Etruscans had spread both north and south, dominating central Italy. In addition, they had their own language, and it is known that women were treated equally, being allowed, like men, to own property and gain an education.

A nineteenth-century illustration depicts Hannibal riding an elephant while the Carthaginians attack Roman troops during the Punic War (264–241 BC). The Sicilian city of Messina appealed to both Carthage and Rome for help against attacks from Syracuse. Although the Carthaginians arrived in Messina first, the Romans invaded the city and ejected them. The Carthaginians returned with more forces, thereby starting the first of the Punic Wars.

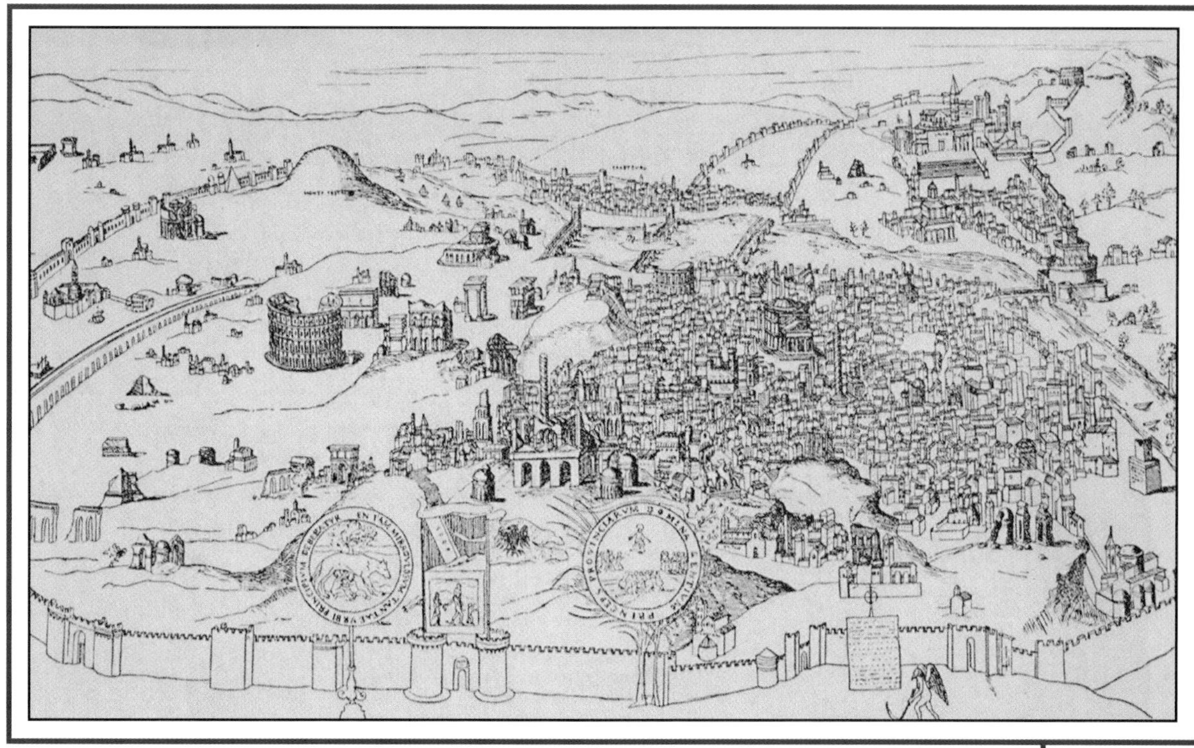

Dating from the 1800s, this illustration depicts the Napoleonic army entering Venice. Napoléon conquered the city of Venice in 1797 and again in 1805. In 1797, Venice became part of Austria after the signing of the Treaty of Campo Formio between Napoléon and Count Ludwig von Cobenzl.

Around 500 BC, the Etruscan civilization began to decline, driven by the Celts who attacked from the north, Greeks who attacked from the south, and Romans who revolted from within. By 250 BC, the Etruscan culture had disappeared completely.

The Roman Republic

Most of what is known about Italy's ancient peoples and history begins with the Romans. While the Greeks were settling southern Italy and Sicily, a group of people called the Latins (later the Romans) began settling in the northern and central regions. The city of Rome originated on the banks of the Tiber River. According to legend, the city of Rome was founded in 753 BC by Romulus and Remus, twin sons of Mars, the Roman god of war. This legend, which is recounted in detail in chapter four of this book, has enjoyed great popularity over the centuries and endures as an entertaining account of the birth of Rome. More likely, shepherds and farmers settled the area and established the city.

Emerging as the dominant cultural group on the Italian peninsula, the Romans unified its various peoples under one rule—the Roman Republic.

Beginning in 509 BC, after ousting their kings, the Roman nobility established a new system of rule, the republic. Two elected leaders called consuls ruled the republic and led the military. Later, a Senate was added to the government system to advise the consuls. Members of the Senate were patricians, or respected citizens from good families. In the beginning, the patricians who were a very small part of the Roman population, monopolized power. However, in response to popular pressure, a tribunal was later formed consisting of citizens from common families and the military.

Julius Caesar

Julius Caesar (100–44 BC), a military genius and accomplished writer and public speaker, rose to power as a government leader and military general in the Roman Republic. He was elected to the position of consul, one of the two main leaders of Roman government. Next, he rose to the position of senior consul, essentially the dictator of Rome, a position he declared was to last for the length of his remaining life. He held this position from 46 BC until his death two years later. As emperor, he directed some of his efforts to reforms such as land redistribution and plans to help unemployed workers. Also, he made all inhabitants of Italy Roman citizens. But the Senate could not accept Caesar as a lifetime dictator. A group of senators, including a man named Brutus, arranged for his assassination on the Ides of March (March 15), a date that some say was prophesized years earlier by the Etruscans. Part of Julius Caesar's legacy to the Roman Empire was that after his death, Roman emperors were known as caesars.

This contemporary sculpture depicts a bust of Julius Caesar, Roman general, statesman, and writer. After Caesar's murder, the conspirators had no strategy to restore the Roman Republic. They were unprepared for the death's aftermath, namely the lack of faith in the government by the people, and as a result, thirteen years of civil war continued.

The Roman Empire

The Roman Republic became the Roman Empire when, in 27 BC, Augustus Caesar (63 BC–AD 14) declared himself dictator. Following Julius Caesar's murder, the empire was ruled by Octavian Caesar, who took the name Augustus ("the revered") and became

Daily Life in Rome

Although life for wealthy Romans was extravagant and civilized, life for Roman slaves was difficult and short. As rich Romans enjoyed lavish meals, slaves lived in small apartments and ate corn that was provided by the government. Although women often managed the slaves, the man was the true leader of the household. Together, most families went to temples where they made sacrifices to the gods.

Inside the villas of wealthy Romans were new levels of comfort and beauty. Some homes had as many as twenty rooms with skylights, private gardens, and indoor toilets. Tile floors heated from beneath by circulating hot water and steam was channeled through walls to create primitive indoor heating. On the walls, detailed fresco paintings brightened the rooms.

Mosaic, a form of tile work, was widely used to create beautiful floors in homes, temples, baths, and courtyards. Over a base of concrete, small colorful pieces of tile, stone, marble, and glass called *tesserae* were set in plaster. The pieces were arranged to form shapes, scenes from everyday life, people and animals, and gods and goddesses. When the plaster dried, the colored patterns were permanent and durable. In fact, many mosaics have survived to this day.

For the public, bathhouses were built with an elaborate web of rooms and gardens, often with slaves to serve the rich. Other rooms were used for exercise, games, and saunas. The rooms and baths were heated with steam from furnaces, carried through a network of channels called a hypocaust. One such public bath in Rome is the Baths of Caracalla, built between AD 206 and 216.

The wealthy also enjoyed attending the theater or the "circus"—gladiator fights where slaves were often pitted against wild animals, or each other.

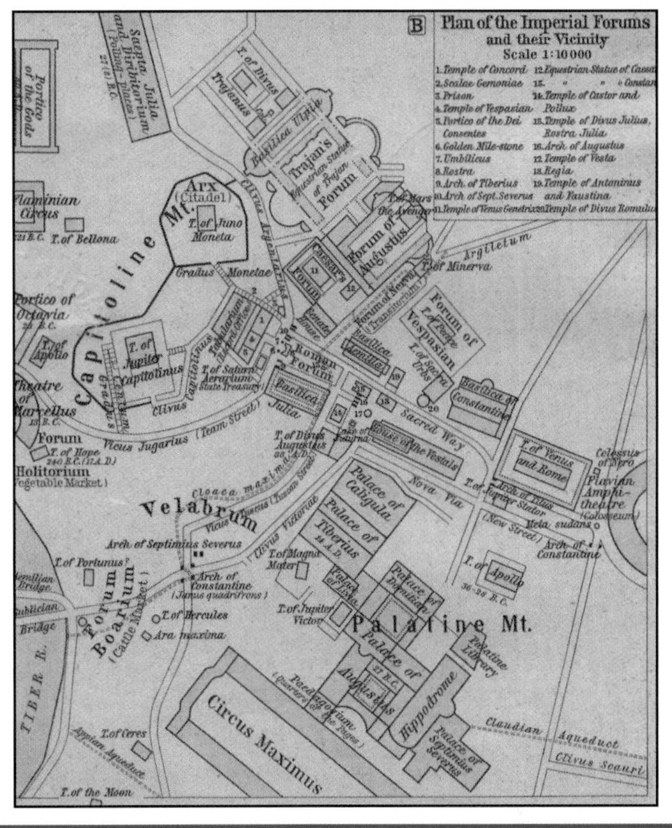

This map, drawn in 1923 as part of *The Historical Atlas*, written by William R. Shepherd, depicts the Roman Forum and its vicinity at the time of the Roman Republic. Several temples, markets, government buildings, and the *tullianum*, or prison, may also be seen.

the first Roman emperor. This time of peace in Roman history is commonly referred to as *Pax Romana*, or "Roman Peace." At this time, the empire's territories were vast. Since about 200 BC, Rome had controlled most of Italy. Meanwhile, the empire had gained control of nearby islands. Within a few hundred years, the Romans dominated the entire Mediterranean region. During the Punic War, Rome conquered the Phoenician city of Carthage in North Africa, in present-day Tunisia. To the west they conquered Gaul as well, which was most of western Europe. Still farther west they conquered Britannia, known today as the United Kingdom. The Romans also pushed into the Middle East. At the end of the first century AD, the Roman Empire reached its peak. By AD 285, the Roman emperor Diocletian (245–313) divided Roman territories into two parts: the eastern Byzantine Empire and the western Roman Empire.

But the entire empire's power, while great, was not everlasting. Early in the fifth century, Barbarian tribes from the Far East began to invade the Roman Empire's fringes. Within the heart of Rome, disagreements arose over how to handle the new challenges, further weakening Roman power. Invasions from the north increasingly tested the empire's strength. By AD 410, the Visigoths sacked Rome. Then the Huns,

The Roman Forum holds two great historical buildings, the Temple of Castor and Pollux and the Temple of Vesta. King Tarquinius Priscus created the Roman Forum in 600 BC as a marketplace, which eventually expanded with the Roman Empire and became the center of political, religious, and commercial activity in the ancient world.

This portrait of Cosimo de Medici I dates from the sixteenth century. Medici was known for his generosity to the arts. During his lifetime, he was responsible for issuing the first Latin edition of Plato's works, founding the Medici Library, creating the Platonic Academy for Greek studies, and supporting artists like Brunelleschi, Donatello, and Ghiberti. Under the direction of the Medici family, Florence became the cultural center of Europe.

led by Attila (406?–453), invaded the western Roman Empire in AD 452. Vandals followed. The long-crumbling region finally fell apart in AD 476.

The Renaissance

Following the Middle Ages, territory in Italy changed hands as various invaders from Byzantium, Germany, Arabia, France, Spain, and Austria swept through the region. At this point, Italy was divided into powerful city-states. Many of these states were independent from the northern region controlled by the Lombards, the central region controlled by Charlemagne (742–814) and the Roman Catholic Church, and the southern region controlled by Normans. The period of rebirth that followed the Middle Ages is called the Renaissance, a time when the arts flourished.

The Italian Renaissance, beginning around 1400, inspired a new sense of unity among the peoples of the Italian peninsula. Wealthy and powerful families of the merchant class, developed in part because of the trading successes of nearby Italian port cities such as Naples and Genoa, became patrons of the arts. For the

This illustration appeared in the first printing of *Marco Polo's Travels* in 1477. Marco Polo (1254–1324) was a Venetian merchant, traveler, and author who traveled the Silk Road farther than any of his predecessors. Polo's journey through China lasted twenty-four years. Along the way he became the confidant of Kublai Khan, traveled the whole of China, and returned to share his experiences.

This book illustration of Amerigo Vespucci (1454–1512) dates from the sixteenth century. Vespucci was a famous Italian navigator, who claimed to have made four voyages to the New World. However, some scholars doubt the extent and discoveries of his journeys. Because German mapmaker Martin Waldseemüller believed Vespucci to be the first European to reach the New World, he suggested the continent be named after the explorer in 1507.

first time, a national Italian identity began to emerge, born in part through shared music, sculpture, architecture, painting, and literature.

By the 1520s, the Renaissance began to give way to a time when religious leaders became intolerant of intellectuals—a time known as the Counter Reformation, when the theories of scholars, explorers, and scientists rocked the foundations of the Catholic Church. During this period of torture and fear, Italian intellectuals like the astronomer Galileo Galilei (1564–1642) were persecuted. In the 200 or so years that followed, Italian city-states lost power, and Italy became a land dominated by outsiders such as Spaniards, Austrians, and the French.

Napoléon Bonaparte

In 1796, Napoléon Bonaparte (1769–1821) marched French troops across the Alps into Italy. He defeated the Austro-Hungarians in Lombardy

French artist Jacques-Louis David painted this portrait titled *Napoléon in His Study* in 1812. David was Napoléon's official painter as well as the central figure of the art movement known as Neoclassicism, which was a nineteenth-century French style that utilized the ideals of ancient Greek and Roman art. Neoclassic artists used classic forms to express their visions of courage, sacrifice, and love of country.

During the eighteenth century, liberal ideals concerning a need for a united kingdom spread throughout Europe. It was not until 1848, however, that the first war for independence broke out in Sicily. Because of the pope's control over the Papal States, true independence for Italy did not occur until 1881 when its military defeated Austria and seized control. This is a portrait of Victor Emmanuel II, the first king of a unified Italy.

and moved south across the Ligurian Sea to conquer the Kingdom of Sardinia, forming the Cisalpine Republic. Over the next few years he added more territories to the republic, renaming it the Italian Republic. In 1805, Napoléon was crowned king of Italy. To the south, he formed the Kingdom of Naples where he named his brother the new king. The French controlled the entire Italian peninsula.

Napoléon brought important changes to Italy. In particular, he established a single system of currency and a common system of weights and measures and also unified legal practices under a single legal code. He was also responsible for improving Italy's bridges, roads, and school systems, reforms that inspired the Italian people. As long as Italians cooperated with French rule, they were allowed to take part in local government. Napoléon also demanded that Italian citizens pay taxes and serve in the military.

The movement for a unified Italy resurfaced, coming to a head during the French occupation. With the withdrawal of the French, all of Italy except Rome united in the 1860s. On March 17, 1861, Italians proclaimed the Kingdom of Italy. They appointed their first king, Victor Emmanuel II (1820–1878) of the House of Savoy. Then, in 1870, Rome joined the Italian union. Until 1922, the kingdom was governed as a constitutional monarchy with an elected parliament. Under this arrangement, Italy's main leaders were a monarch (king) and a prime minister, who led the parliament.

Benito Mussolini and the Fascist Era

In 1914, World War I developed in Europe and Russia. When Italy entered the war in 1915, it sided with Great Britain, France, and Russia. Together the four countries—called the Allied Powers—fought Germany and Austria-Hungary. By 1918, the Allies were victorious. Nevertheless, Italians faced much difficulty after the war. Their

Giuseppe Garibaldi

Giuseppe Garibaldi (1807–1882) was born in Nice, a city in the Kingdom of Piedmont-Sardinia. As a young man, Garibaldi supported the revolutionary movement in Sardinia. In 1833, he joined a revolt against the king, but the rebellion failed. Three years later, Garibaldi went to South America. Once there he became a war hero, helping Uruguay win its independence from Argentina. At one point, Garibaldi's troops needed shirts, but he had little money. He took old, blood-stained shirts from butchers and dyed them red for his soldiers. Later, red became the color of the Communist revolution.

In 1848, Garibaldi returned to Italy and helped defend the Roman Republic against the Austrians. Returning to Sardinia in 1854, he became a general in the Piedmontese army. In 1860, Garibaldi gathered 1,000 red-shirted volunteers and led them to drive out the Bourbons from Sicily and Naples. He led the city-states of the Italian peninsula, along with Sardinia and Sicily, to unite under King Victor Emmanuel II. Today in Italy, Garibaldi is remembered as a national hero.

When Benito Mussolini seized power in 1922, he established a youth movement according to the Fascist motto *"largo ai giovani,"* meaning, "Make way for the youth!" Italian boys between the ages of eight and twenty-one were expected to belong to the various youth organizations. These groups led by the Fascist Party began to cultivate a warlike spirit in boys by providing social, military, and sports activities that followed a Fascist ideology. The purpose of these organizations was to train boys to become good soldiers.

country had huge war debts, the land was scarred from battle, and more than 350,000 men had died. The time was right for a new kind of leader to take control of the country and help solve its problems. A young political speaker and writer, Benito Mussolini (1883–1945), believed he could unite the country and solve its problems. The son of a socialist blacksmith, Mussolini had had a troubled childhood during which he stabbed two classmates and was expelled from schools. Early in life, he began to talk about violence as a means to an end.

In 1919, Mussolini and his followers formed a new political force in Milan. The word "fascism" comes from

This photograph of Mussolini at a rally in Genova giving a well-received speech to his followers appeared in the Italian magazine *Il Mattino Illustrato* on May 23, 1938. After World War I, Italy suffered an extreme economic crisis. Many Europeans felt that Mussolini's ability to restore the economy outweighed "rumors" of police brutality. However, after Mussolini's ruthless invasion of Ethiopia, world opinion of the Fascist dictator changed.

Mussolini's political group, *fasci di combattimento*, meaning "fighting bands." Referring to the ancient symbol of Roman authority—an ax head tied tightly in a bundle of elm or birch rods with a red band—Mussolini wanted his political party bound as tightly as the ax and wooden rods.

Fascists believe in strong government control of workers and industry. They believe that violence is an acceptable way to enforce power and meet demands. Mussolini's Fascists' power grew rapidly. In October 1922, Mussolini threatened that if the Italian government were not turned over to the Fascists, they would march on Rome. He assembled thousands of followers and began the march. Before a violent uprising could occur, King Victor Emmanuel III (1869–1947) agreed to Mussolini's demands and named him prime minister. Mussolini began his dictatorship; his title was Il Duce, which means "the Leader." Although King Emmanuel III was officially head of state, he had no real power.

Under Mussolini's leadership, damage from World War I was repaired, jobs were plentiful, and the

This 1936 swastika pin with the heads of Hitler and Mussolini and the inscription *Roma-Berlino* recognized the Rome-Berlin Axis Pact of World War II. The swastika, the oldest cross and emblem in the world, was used as a symbol of good luck before the Nazi regime corrupted its meaning. It forms a combination of four backward L's standing for Luck, Light, Love, and Life. Swastika insignias can also be found in ancient Rome, Grecian cities, on Buddhist idols, and on Chinese coins.

economy grew stronger. But during this time, Italians' personal liberties were gradually taken away. Trade unions and the free press were abolished, and political spies watched citizens closely. There was no free speech, and all political parties except the Fascist Party were outlawed.

Mussolini formed a friendship with another dictator, Adolf Hitler (1889–1945) of Germany. When World War II erupted, Italy joined forces with Germany and Japan against the Allied Powers of the United Kingdom, France, the Soviet Union, and the United States. After the Allies invaded Sicily in 1943, King Emmanuel III removed Mussolini from office and imprisoned him. The

After the fall of Fascism in Italy following World War II, the nation restructured its government and approved a new constitution on December 22, 1947. The constitution (*right*) was reprinted in this Italian newspaper, and the first part of Article One translates as, "Italy is a Democratic Republic, founded on work." A crowd *(above)* gathered to hear Benito Mussolini declare war on the Allied Powers. Mussolini waited until the defeat of France before declaring war in June 1940, hoping to join Germany, share in its victories, and build a new Roman Empire. Italy's economy and military, however, were not strong enough to support a lengthy conflict. After Italy's defeat in Greece and North Africa, Mussolini instead became a puppet for Hitler's Germany rather than a leader of an Italian empire.

COSTITUZIONE DELLA REPUBBLICA ITALIANA

IL CAPO PROVVISORIO DELLO STATO

Vista la deliberazione dell'Assemblea Costituente, che nella seduta del 22 dicembre 1947 approvato la Costituzione della Repubblica Italiana;

Vista la XVIII disposizione finale della Costituzione;

PROMULGA

la Costituzione della Repubblica Italiana nel seguente testo:

PRINCIPÎ FONDAMENTALI

Art. 1.

L'Italia è una Repubblica democratica, fondata sul lavoro.

La sovranità appartiene al popolo, che la esercita nelle forme e nei limiti della Costituzione.

Art. 2.

La Repubblica riconosce e garantisce i diritti inviolabili dell'uomo, sia come singolo sia nelle formazioni sociali ove si svolge la sua personalità, e richiede l'adempimento dei doveri inderogabili di solidarietà politica, economica e sociale.

Art. 3.

Tutti i cittadini hanno pari dignità sociale e sono eguali davanti alla legge, senza distinzione di sesso, di razza, di lingua, di religione, di opinioni politiche, di condizioni personali e sociali.

E' compito della Repubblica rimuovere gli ostacoli di ordine economico e sociale, che, limitando di fatto la libertà e l'eguaglianza dei cittadini, impediscono il pieno sviluppo della persona umana e l'effettiva partecipazione di tutti i lavoratori all'organizzazione politica, economica e sociale del Paese.

Art. 4.

La Repubblica riconosce a tutti i cittadini il diritto al lavoro e promuove le condizioni che rendano effettivo questo diritto.

Ogni cittadino ha il dovere di svolgere, secondo le proprie possibilità e la propria scelta, un'attività o una funzione che concorra al progresso materiale o spirituale della società.

Art. 5.

La Repubblica, una e indivisibile, riconosce e promuove le autonomie locali; attua nei servizi che dipendono dallo Stato il più ampio decentramento amministrativo; adegua i principî ed i metodi della sua legislazione alle esigenze dell'autonomia e del decentramento.

Art. 6.

La Repubblica tutela con apposite norme le minoranze linguistiche.

Art. 7.

Lo Stato e la Chiesa cattolica sono, ciascuno nel proprio ordine, indipendenti e sovrani.

I loro rapporti sono regolati dai Patti Lateranensi. Le modificazioni dei Patti, accettate dalle due parti, non richiedono procedimento di revisione costituzionale

Art. 8.

Tutte le confessioni religiose sono egualmente libere davanti alla legge.

Le confessioni religiose diverse dalla cattolica hanno diritto di organizzarsi secondo i propri statuti, in quanto non contrastino con l'ordinamento giuridico italiano

Members of the Italian Constituent Assembly approved a new constitution for the Italian Republic by a vote of 453 to 62. Under the new laws Enrico de Nicola (center) became the first president of the republic in 1946. De Nicola (1877–1959) graduated from the University of Naples and practiced criminal law. As one of Italy's most esteemed penal lawyers, he was elected as a deputy in 1909, which started his political career. During the rise of Fascism, he retired from politics. In 1944 de Nicola returned as the most influential mediator for the creation of "lieutenant." In 1946, de Nicola was elected as provisionary head of state, until Luigi Einaudi took office in 1948.

king then appointed Pietro Badoglio (1871–1956) as prime minister. Italy changed loyalties during the war and declared war on Germany. Germany invaded Italy, freeing Mussolini. But in 1945, German forces were driven out. Mussolini was assassinated in April of that year. Later in 1945, World War II ended.

In 1946, Italians voted to end rule by monarchy and elected an assembly to prepare plans for a republic. From 1946 to 1948, Enrico De Nicola served as provisional (temporary) head of state. Then, in 1948, Italy's first president, Luigi Einaudi, took office. Italy has since been governed by a president and parliament.

Modern Italy

In 2002, Italy's population was just under 58 million people, a vast number for its overall size. Nearly 500 people per square

This group of Italian women relax on an outdoor bench. The role of women in Italy is changing. Women are becoming entrepreneurs at a higher rate than men, a figure that increased by 25 percent in 2002. Companies run by women are concentrated in the textile, footwear, and food production industries.

mile (about 200 per square kilometer) pack the land. This is the fifth-highest population density in Europe. Italy's total population is made up of more females (29.7 million) than males (28 million).

Nearly 1.5 million of Italy's residents are immigrants from other countries. According to the Italian National Statistical Institute, in the year 2000, 2.5 percent of residents were immigrants. In January of 2001, immigration had increased 15.3 percent over the previous year. A large number of these immigrants are illegal and come in particular from Albania, Yugoslavia, and Turkey. A large majority of the immigrants choose to live in Italy's northern regions. Less than one-third of the immigrants live in the central regions; even fewer live in the south. Italy's location in the Mediterranean Sea makes it an ideal gateway into Europe for immigrants from Africa. Immigration to Italy continues to be strong.

Traditionally, Italy has also been a land of emigrants, with Italians leaving for work in the United States, Argentina, Brazil, Australia, and Canada. Southern Italians have also moved north in large numbers to work in the factories there.

Quoniam quidē intelligere ⁊ scire cōtingit circa omnes sciētias: quarum sūt principia cause ⁊ elemēta ex horum cognitione. Tūc enim opinamur cognoscere vnūquodq₃: qum causas primas cognoscim⁹: ⁊ principia prima: ⁊ vsq₃ ad elementa. Manifestum quidē quot ⁊ que sunt circa principia sciētie q̄ de natura est prius determinare tētandū.

Quoniam dispositio scientie: ⁊ certitudinis in omnibus vijs habētibus principia: ⁊ causas ⁊ elemēta: nō acquirit nisi ex cognitione istorū. Credimus eni in vnaquaq₃ rerum ipsam scire: qum sciuerimus causas eius simplices: ⁊ prima principia eius: donec perueniamus ad elemēta eius. Manifestū est q̄ in sciētia naturali etiā oportet primo querere determinationem principiorū eius.

Cō. I. Incepit hunc librū a causa propter quā fuit cōsideratio hu⁹ sciētie in cognitione causarū rerū naturaliū: ⁊ dixit: qm̄ dispositio. i. q̄a declaratū est in posteriorib⁹ q̄ dispositio sciētie certe in oībus artib⁹ demonstratiuis ꝯsiderātib⁹ de rebus habētibus vnā quatuor causaꝝ: aut plures vna: aut omnes: nō acquirit nisi ex cognitione causarū. ⁊ nō intēdebat per sciētiā ⁊ certitudinem nomina synonyma: qm̄ noia synonyma nō vtitur i doctrina demonstratiua: sed intendebat dispositionē sciētie certe ⁊ est sciētia pfecta. Sciētia eni alia est pfecta: ⁊ est illa que est p causam: alia est impfecta: ⁊ est illa que ē sine causa. ⁊ intēdebat p vias artes speculatiuas: q̄ dicunt vie q̄a cōsiderans in eis vadit a determinatis rebus ad res indeterminatas ⁊ p res terminatas. ⁊ dixit pncipia: aut causas: aut elemēta: q̄a artiū speculatiuarū aut suarū partiū sunt quedā q̄ ꝯsiderāt de reb⁹ simplicib⁹ carentib⁹ pncipijs ⁊ hec est dispositio sciētie ꝯsiderātis de primis pncipijs cuiuslibet entis. ⁊ dixit principia: aut causas: aut elemēta ꝓpter diuersitatē modorū q̄tuor causaꝝ. ⁊ intēdebat p principia in hoc loco causas agētes ⁊ mouētes: ⁊ p causas: fines: ⁊ p elementa causas q̄ sūt ptes rei. s. materiā ⁊ formā ⁊ q̄ hic vtit hoc noie principiū ꝓprie: ⁊ simili hoc nomie causa: q̄a sūt nomia synonyma qum vtitur cōiter. ⁊ sicut mihi videt exposuit ipse Alex. ⁊ intēdebat Aris. per hūc sermonē docere q̄ nō oēs artes ꝯsiderāt de omnib⁹ causis: sed quedā ꝯsiderāt de causa formali tm̄. s. mathematice: ⁊ quedā de trib⁹ causis. s. motore: ⁊ forma: ⁊ fine: ⁊ est sciētia diuina. ⁊ quedā de q̄tuor causis: ⁊ est sciētia nālis: ⁊ q̄a hoc nō fuit manifestū in hoc loco: induxit sermonē in forma dubitatiōis: ⁊ .d. hn̄tibus principia: aut causas: aut elementa. i. qm̄ idē sequit siue ponat q̄ ille res habeāt principia agētia: aut finalia: aut elemētaria: aut oia: ⁊ impossibile est ut hec cōiunctio aut sit sicut copulatiua: nā dispositio certe scie inuenit in reb⁹ hn̄tibus causas quasdā p sciētiā illarū causarū: sicut inuenit in hn̄tib⁹ oēs causas. ⁊ qū posuit hāc ꝓpositionē induxit testimoniū ad verificandū illā: q̄ fere induxit in posteriorib⁹ analecticis: ⁊ .d. credimus eni in vnaquaq₃ rerū ⁊c. ⁊ signū eius q̄d dixim⁹ q̄ dispositio scie certe de aliq̄ nō acquirit nisi ex cognitiōe cause cui⁹ est: qm̄ oīs qui dicit se scire aliq̄d: nō dicit hoc nisi qn̄ sciuerit illud p suas oēs causas ꝓpinquas ⁊ remotas: ⁊ hoc inuenit in omī qui aliq̄d scit in veritate: aut fm existimationē: ⁊ q̄ in ista ꝓpositione ꝯueniūt oēs ꝯsiderātes adeo q̄ etiā sophiste ut dixit in posteriorib⁹. D. d. qum sciuerimus causas eius simplices: ⁊ intendit ut videt causas existētes in re primas nō cōpositas: ⁊ sūt prima mā: ⁊ vltima forma. que eni sunt pret primā materiā ⁊ vltimā formā cuiuslibet rerū nāliū: sūt materie cōposite: ⁊ forme cōposite. D. d. ⁊ prima principia: ⁊ intēdit h ut videt p prima principia: primas causas q̄ sūt extra rem. s. primū agens: ⁊ vltimū finē omniū rerū. D. d. donec pueniam⁹ ad elementa eius: ⁊ intēdit h p elemēta causas existētes in re propinquas ⁊ essentiales. ⁊ innuit p hoc q̄d dixit: q̄ doctrina ordinata est incipe a cognitione causarū primarū rei cognoscende pfecte. Deinde intēdere ad cognitionē aliarū causarum remotarū fm ordinē: donec pueniat ad causas ꝓpinquas: ⁊ fm hoc vtit h hoc noie causa: ⁊ elementū alio mō ab eo q̄ vsus est illic pus fm suū morē in habēdo modicā sollicitudinē de nominib⁹. ⁊ qum posuit hāc maiorē ꝓpositionē in hoc sermone. s. dicente q̄ scientia certa de rebus habētibus causas ⁊ elemēta nō acquirit nisi ex cognitiōe causarū ⁊ elementorū eorū: dimisit minorē ꝓpositionē: ⁊ induxit cōclusionē quā intēdit p hūc sermonē: ⁊ dixit manifestum est q̄ in sciētia nāli ⁊c. i. manifestū est: qm̄ ex hoc sequit q̄ qui vult largiri sciētiā de natura oportet ipsum prius querere determinationē causarū rerū nāliū habētium causas ⁊ elemēta. ⁊ iste sermo cōponit sic: oia nālia habent causas ⁊ elemēta: ⁊ oia habētia causas ⁊ elemēta nō sciunt nisi ex cognitione causarū ⁊ elementorū: ergo omnia nālia nō sciunt nisi ex cognitione suarū cārū ⁊ elemētorū.

Innata est autē via ex notiorib⁹ nobis ⁊ certioribus incertiora nature ⁊ notiora: nō enim sūt eadem nobis nota ⁊ simpliciter. vnde quidē necesse est fm hunc modū ꝓcedere ex incertiorib⁹ nature: nobis autē certioribus incertiora nature ⁊ notiora.

Et via ad illa est de rebus notioribus ⁊ ma-

A A 2

THE LANGUAGE OF ITALY

3

From Ancient Latin to Modern Italian

Italians are passionate about self-expression. Their conversations are spirited, and they gesture frequently with their hands to emphasize a point. Some people even say that Italians' hands have a language all their own.

Long ago, in the days of the Roman Empire, the primary language was Latin. Formal Latin was used for public speaking and official occasions, and a more casual form of Latin was used in everyday speech and at home. Today, Italy's national language is Italian, which developed from the less formal Latin. Most natives of Italy speak Italian. However, some may be more familiar with variations of Italian spoken in different regions of the country.

Because of its Latin roots, Italian is classified as a romance language, much like French, Spanish, and Portuguese, among others. Some of these languages sound alike. For example, sometimes Spanish speakers are able to understand Italian speakers—not because they have learned Italian—but because of the close similarity of the two languages.

Aristotle's *Opera* was reprinted in 1483 with a frontispiece (*left*) illustrated by Girolamo da Cremona. Da Cremona worked as a manuscript illuminator throughout Italy and ended his career illustrating books. The Roman graffiti seen in the photograph *(above)* was discovered in Pompeii, an ancient city that was destroyed by volcanic eruptions in AD 79. A port city located on the Bay of Naples, Pompeii became famous 1,700 years after its tragic end when its amphitheater was discovered in 1748. Roman graffiti such as this often described upcoming gladiator fights or messages of gossip.

Say It in Italian

ciao!	(CHAOW)	hello!
buon giorno	(bwohn JOHR-noh)	hello, good day
per favore	(pehr fah-VOR-ay)	please
arrivederci	(ah-ree-veh-DEHR-chee)	good-bye, see you soon
scuola	(sko-OH-lah)	school
piazza	(pe-AHT-zah)	town square
grazie	(GRAH-zeh)	thank you
come sta?	(KOH-may STAH)	how are you?
molto bene	(MOHL-toh BEH-neh)	very well

Varied Dialects

Although Italian is the official language of Italy, different regions of the country speak their own dialects. A dialect is a version of language used in one particular section of a country. It uses words, pronunciation, and grammar a little differently than dialects in other regions. The national language is a combination of all the dialects taken together.

This diversity in speaking reaches back to the earliest days of Italy's history, when various cultures settled the land. High mountain ranges prevented villagers from much travel to other regions. As a result, each village or area developed its own unique culture, including its own methods of speaking. Often, people living in one region could not understand people living in a different region. A national language did not take hold until after the kingdom of Italy was established in 1861. Even today, some Italians prefer their regional dialect to standard Italian. For example, on the island of Sicily, Sicilian is commonly spoken, as is Sardinian on Sardinia.

Italian continues to evolve with use because it is a "living" language. For example, standard, formal Italian was originally based on Tuscan Italian, which included a mixture of dialects from Tuscany. In more recent times, widespread access to radios, television, film, and newspapers has brought bits of other dialects

A passerby stops to talk to some men sitting on a sidewalk bench in Scanno, a small Italian town with a population of only two thousand. Today, a majority of Italians speak official Italian, making regional dialects less obvious. However, there are two bilingual regions in Italy where Italian is used alongside French and German. A 1948 statute allows for French and Italian to be used in the Aosta Valley region and German and Italian to be used as the official languages of the Trentino Alto Adige region.

into the language standard. Today, official Italian includes bits of dialects from regions such as Rome, Milan, and Turin in addition to the Tuscan dialect.

The Italian alphabet contains twenty-one letters—most letters of the English alphabet. The letters J, K, W, X, and Y are not found in Italian.

Foreign words have also become mixed into the everyday speech of Italians. For example, in Calabria, speakers sprinkle their language with Greek words left over from ancient times when Greeks settled the region. Along the northern border, Italians near France speak French, and those near Austria speak German. A few foreign languages introduced into Italy by immigrants include Albanian, Serbo-Croatian, and Occitan (from southern France). Many English words have been derived from Italian, such as ballot, bandit, broccoli,

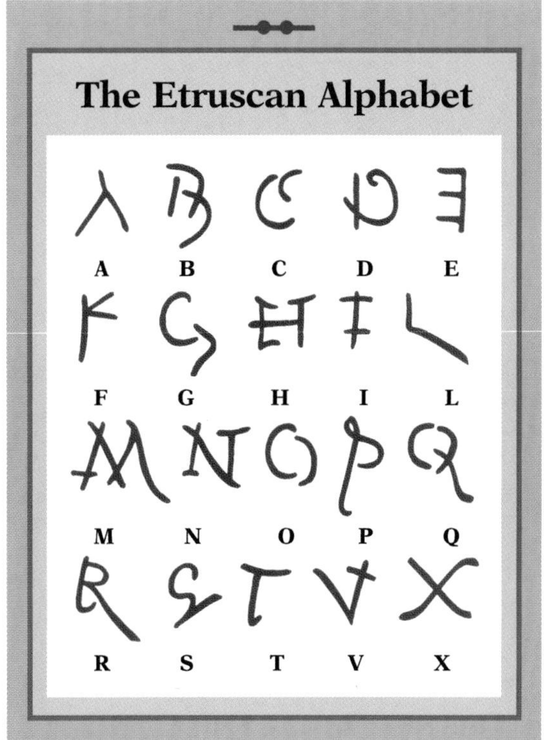

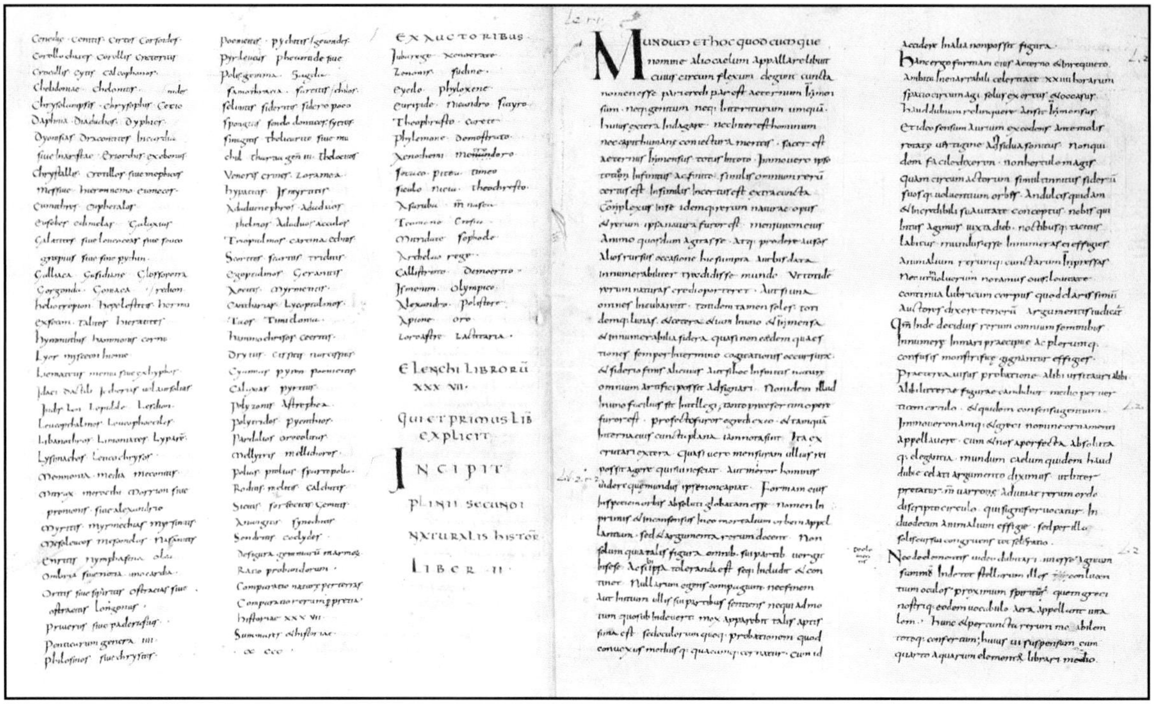

The manuscript pages featured on this page are from *Historia Naturalis*, written by Gaius Plinius Secundus, known as Pliny the Elder, in AD 77. His book covers a variety of subjects such as cosmology, astronomy, and agriculture, and he recorded Latin synonyms for Greek plants, which made identifying flora in Greek writing possible. In AD 79, Pliny the Elder died in the volcanic eruption in Pompeii.

graffiti, pizza, prima donna, trio, umbrella, violin, and volcano. Words for popular products from the United States, such as the names of soft drinks and fast foods, and words like "jeans," have likewise become common in Italian.

Written Communication

Italy developed a system of writing from inventions made by several other world civilizations. The Chinese, for instance, developed the first techniques of printing and papermaking, methods adopted by the Arabs around AD 751. By way of trade routes between Europe, Asia, and Africa, these techniques soon came to Italy. In the days before the printing press, scribes painstakingly copied passages by hand onto parchment or calfskin. The pages were often illustrated elaborately and decorated in brightly colored inks. The beautiful colors illuminated the plain black text. For this reason, these early books are called illuminated manuscripts.

NICOLAI
MACHIAVELLI
PRINCEPS.

EX
SYLVESTRI TELII
FVLGINATIS TRADVCTIONE
diligenter emendata.

Adiecta sunt eiusdem argumenti, Aliorum quorundam contra Machiauellum scripta de potestate & officio Principum, & contra tyrannos.

BASILEAE
Ex officina Petri Pernae.
M D XXC.

A Latin translation of the book *Il Principe* (*The Prince*) by Italian political theorist and writer Niccolò Machiavelli was written in 1513. In the book, he offered guidance to Lorenzo de Medici for maintaining control over Florence and uniting Italy as a republic. However, his advice was misinterpreted and it earned him the reputation of an amoral and cynical man associated with a corrupt government. Today, the word Machiavellian means marked by cunning, duplicity, or bad faith.

Then, in Germany in the mid-1400s, Johannes Gutenberg (1390–1468) created a printing press that used movable type. The stage was set for a new subculture in Italy—the reading public.

By the 1460s, Italian publishers began using Gutenberg's technology to produce their own printed pages. By using a printing press, for the first time many copies of a work could be printed and then distributed easily to a number of people. The path was paved for novelists, philosophers, politicians, teachers, and other writers to share their words with masses of people. For example, *The Divine Comedy*, written by Dante (also known as Dante Alighieri, 1265–1321) was the first major work of literature in Italian. Written between 1308 and 1312, the three-volume poem about hell, purgatory, and paradise was very long. It was not until the printing press made copying faster and easier that Dante's work become available to large numbers of readers. The majority of the first books printed in Italy, and in Venice in particular, included major Greek and Roman works of antiquity.

Along with the works of great authors, the myths and legends from Italy's long history could now be printed and bound much more easily than before. Although the task of recording and printing the vast number of stories was not fast or easy, over time, Italy's classic stories were printed.

ITALIAN MYTHS AND LEGENDS

4

Much of Italy's rich history of myth and legend centers on the Romans. In myths, Romans expressed their beliefs about the wonders and dangers of the world in which they lived. While modern readers see myths as fanciful stories of make-believe gods and goddesses, Romans believed in these deities with a religious faith. In this regard, many of Italy's myths are part of its religious history. Roman legends, on the other hand, explained the origins of their customs, ancient leaders, and cities. For example, the legend of Romulus and Remus tells the story of how Rome was founded. Although Italy's legends cannot be taken as fact, they do provide fascinating accounts of traditional beliefs about the country's past.

Roman Gods

Numina, a word meaning "powers," is the name for the oldest of Roman gods. Numina served useful purposes in Roman culture. For example, the One Who Guards the Cradle watched over infants; Pales was the Strengthener of Cattle; and Sylvanus was the Helper of Plowmen and Woodcutters. There were many of these Numina. Unlike later gods, the Numina had no specific appearance, nor were they defined as male or female.

Dating from 360 BC, this design *(left)* from an Etruscan red-figure bell crater details Hera in ornate dress and holding a scepter, turning toward Hercules. Much of the form and design of Etruscan pottery reflects earlier Greek works. Located in the atrium of the House of Vettii, this mural *(above)* is a shrine to household gods. In its center stands the Genius with a veiled head for sacrifice and flanked by two Lares. Wealthy merchant brothers owned this house in AD 62, which has been preserved as an excellent example of property owned by the commercial middle class.

Roman Gods and Goddesses

Jupiter	Chief god; god of the sky
Juno	Goddess of marriage, childbirth, and women; wife of Jupiter
Minerva	Goddess of wisdom and crafts; daughter of Jupiter
Vesta	Goddess of the hearth (fireplace); sister to Jupiter
Neptune	God of the sea; brother to Jupiter
Mars	God of war; son of Jupiter and Juno
Venus	Goddess of love and beauty; mother of Cupid; daughter of Jupiter
Mercury	Messenger of the gods; god of trade; son of Jupiter
Diana	Goddess of the moon, hunting, and fertility; daughter of Jupiter
Vulcan	God of fire; son of Juno
Apollo	God of the sun, music, and the arts; son of Jupiter
Pluto	God of the underworld; god of wealth; brother to Jupiter
Ceres	Goddess of the harvest
Bacchus	God of wine and parties
Saturn	God of farming and of weights and measures

Of all the Numina, the most important were the Lares and Penates. Each family had its own Lar, which was the spirit of an ancestor. In addition, the family had several gods of the fireside and storehouses, called Penates. The entire household entrusted its safety and protection to these family gods. A portion of food at each meal was set aside to honor them. In a similar manner, each city had its own Lares and Penates, which were believed to protect it in the same way that others protected the household.

As the Roman Republic (and later Roman Empire) grew, Romans accepted foreign religions or cults. Adopted from conquered peoples, the beliefs became part of Roman culture. Some of the most well-known Roman gods and goddesses were adapted from Greek deities but given Roman names. A rich history of storytelling developed around the Roman gods and goddesses. The chief of the gods was Jupiter, and his wife was Juno. Most of the other main gods and goddesses were related to one or both of these two.

The Romans built temples to honor particular gods, many times creating a statue of the god that would be placed inside the structure.

This bronze statue of the Roman god Jupiter dates from the first or second century. In Roman mythology, Jupiter, god of the sky and chief of the Roman pantheon of gods, is the Roman equivalent to the Greek god Zeus.

According to tradition, the god lived inside the statue, so the statue was set facing the door so the god could "see" what went on outside. In the courtyard, in view of the statue, sacrifices were made and gifts were offered. Three important temples stood on Capitoline Hill in Rome. These were built for Jupiter, Juno, and Minerva. Other temples were built for Diana, Ceres, Apollo, Saturn, and other deities.

A temple founded for Vesta had special traditions. Young unmarried women, referred to as vestal virgins, spent thirty years of their lives serving in the temple. Vesta was the keeper of a pure fire symbolizing life. In her temple, the most important duty of the vestal virgins was to keep the sacred flame burning continuously. These women, sometimes called priestesses, were not allowed to marry during the time they served in the temple. If a vestal virgin broke her sacred vows, she was buried alive.

Myths and Customs

In addition to building temples, Romans practiced special customs in honor of gods and goddesses. On July 23, they held a festival in honor of Neptune, god of the seas, who could summon raging storms or smooth the waters into calmness. On February 15, they held a wild festival called *Lupercalia*. It was in honor of Faunus, the half-man, half-goat son of Jupiter. During this strange festival, men chased young women through the streets and struck at them with whips. To the Romans, this action was a symbol of keeping away infertility. On March 1, they celebrated the festival of *Matronalia*, in honor of Juno, after whom the month of June is named.

This Roman mosaic illustrates Orpheus with a lyre sitting in a circle of Acanthus leaves. In Roman mythology, Orpheus's music was irresistible. With a pluck of his instrument, he could charm birds, trees, and even mountains. A lyre is an ancient Greek stringed instrument that accompanied song and recitation. This mosaic of Orpheus is one of many that were found at an archaeological site in Dougga, Tunisia, on the northern African coast, which was an ancient Roman city during the fourth century BC.

Other months named after Roman deities are January, named after Janus (god of doors and new beginnings); March, named after Mars; and May, named after Maia, the goddess of growth.

In some cases, the myths helped explain the workings of the natural world. For example, to explain why the seasons change during the year, the story of Proserpine (sometimes spelled Persephone) was told. Pluto, god of the underworld, kidnapped Proserpine, daughter of Ceres. Heartbroken at the loss of her daughter, Ceres asked the chief god, Jupiter, to force Pluto to return Proserpine. Instead, Jupiter compromised with Pluto. For nine months of the year, Proserpine could live above ground with Ceres. But for the other three months, she would live in the underworld as Pluto's queen. The three months when Proserpine lives in the underworld are during the winter. Her first three happy months of freedom above ground are spring. Summer is next. Then, during the three months when her time in the underworld grows rapidly closer, autumn comes to the land.

Looking to the night sky, Romans saw evidence of their gods in the stars. The god Apollo once gave a beautiful lyre, or harp, to a human named Orpheus. Orpheus's skill on the lyre was so wonderful that he charmed all of nature with his music. Wild beasts became tame and rivers changed course to follow the sound of his playing. After Orpheus died, his lyre was placed in the heavens as the constellation Lyra.

Cupid, the god of love, is celebrated in modern times as part of the festivities of St. Valentine's Day. But this holiday actually has its origins in the lives of two Christian martyrs, Valentine of Rome and Valentine of Interamna (modern-day Terni, a city in central Italy). Historians believe that these two Valentines may have actually been the same person. At any rate, the tradition of a lovers' feast has been practiced on this day since the fourteenth century. Today, St. Valentine's Day is celebrated on February 14.

Italian Legends Retold for Modern Readers

Tomie dePaola (1934–) is a popular writer and illustrator of children's stories. As someone who loves the old legends of Italy, he has retold some of them in English for modern readers. Some of his books are *The Legend of Old Befana*, *The Prince of the Dolomites*, and *Strega Nona: An Old Tale*. One of his most popular story characters is Strega Nona, which means "Grandma Witch" in Italian.

In addition, dePaola uses his artistic skills to create illustrations for Italian legends. For example, he provided artwork for *The Mysterious Giant of Barletta*, which he also wrote, based on a classic Italian folktale.

DePaola, who is of Italian and Irish descent, was born in Meriden, Connecticut, in 1934. A storyteller and artist for nearly forty years, dePaola has written or illustrated more than 200 books. His work has won many awards, including a Caldecott Honor Award, a Newbery Honor Award, and the Smithson Medal.

Cultural Influences

Besides adopting Greek gods, Roman culture also absorbed the gods and religions of other ancient cultures. One such culture is that of the Etruscans, a people who worshiped nature. They believed in many gods and goddesses and thought that these deities communicated through nature. In order to learn the gods' will and wishes, the Etruscans studied the stars and the weather. They saw religious meaning in lightning. They studied the spilled intestines of sacrificed animals. They looked for meaning in their dreams.

Later, during the Roman era, similar beliefs were common. Some would call these beliefs superstitions. For example, it was considered good luck if a person saw bees or snakes. But for a man or woman who heard the hoot of an owl, or tripped and fell in the street, bad luck was to be expected. Superstitious beliefs about magic and witchcraft were part of the culture, too. Many people visited witches or sorceresses to obtain special potions. They used the potions in attempts to make others appreciate them, to punish enemies, or for numerous other reasons. Other people consulted astrologers who studied the stars and made predictions about the future. And to many Romans, ghosts were also very real.

The Legend of Rome

One of the most well-known Italian legends tells the story of the founding of Rome in 753 BC. Twin baby brothers, Romulus and Remus, were born to a woman named Silvia. The infants were in great danger from their city's ruler, who saw them as rivals to his throne. To save the twins, Silvia placed them in a basket and set it afloat on the Tiber River. When the basket came to rest on the banks of the river, a she-wolf took the boys and cared for them. The wolf's name is often said to be Capitoline. When they were older, a shepherd found them and took them home, where he and his wife raised them. One day, they were visited by a fabulous being who said he was Mars, the god of war. Mars told them he was their father.

Years later, Romulus and Remus returned to the spot where they had been rescued by the wolf. There, on the banks of the Tiber, they laid the plans for a city, each brother marking off the location of its walls. Unfortunately, the brothers fought over how to share ruling power of the city. During one of their clashes, Romulus killed Remus and became the first ruler of Rome, a city he named after himself.

The Story of the Epiphany

Another Italian legend, the story of *La Befana*, tells a story of the Epiphany—a religious festival in honor of the three wise men, known as the Magi, who brought gifts to the infant Jesus. On the eve of the Epiphany, La Befana is said to bring gifts to the children of Italy. The legend, which originally took place during the time of the birth of the baby Jesus, is popularly told around the time

This bronze sculpture, entitled *She-Wolf of the Capital*, circa 500 BC, was created by a Roman sculptor to honor Romulus and Remus, the legendary sibling founders of Rome who were abandoned and raised by a she-wolf. According to the legend, Romulus killed Remus and ruled Rome alone, proving himself as a great leader in peace and war. Ancient Romans believed he resided in heaven, and worshiped him under the name of Quirinus.

Italian painter, sculptor, and architect Giotto di Bondone is recognized as the first master of art during the Italian Renaissance. The illustration titled *The Adoration of the King* is one of thirty-eight frescoes Bondone painted in the Arena Chapel in Padua in 1305. The frescoes depict scenes from the lives of Mary and Christ.

of the Christian religious festival of the Epiphany. The name of the old woman in the story, Befana, comes from the Italian word for Epiphany, *epifania*.

As the legend goes, La Befana was an old woman living alone in a small house in the hills of Italy. She spent her days baking and sweeping. On their way to visit the baby Jesus, the Magi stopped at her house and asked her for directions. She could not help them. Although they invited La Befana to join them on their journey, she stayed home. Later, she wished she had gone with the three wise men. Bearing gifts and her broom (to help Jesus' mother clean), she set out on her own journey to find the Christ child. Unfortunately, try as she might, she could not find him. She continues searching to this day. Each year on the eve of the Epiphany, she visits the houses where children live, hoping to find baby Jesus within. Since she loves all children, she leaves gifts for them in each house before moving on in her search.

42
40
=2
21-
10=
11

ITALIAN FESTIVALS AND CEREMONIES OF ANTIQUITY AND TODAY

5

Italy is a festive country. Throughout the year, Italians celebrate many festivals and holidays with their families, communities, and churches. The celebrations are marked by masses of people, fabulous foods, and high spirits. Fireworks may add sparkle to a night scene. Some of the festivals are religious, some are family oriented, and a few are political. Others reflect ancient traditions.

Religious Festivals and Holidays

Religious festivals include *feste*, which are days to honor the Catholic saints. As part of the celebration, children may dress in traditional costumes. Huge processions take place, and statues of the saints are carried through the streets. As with most other festivals and holidays, Italians enjoy traditional foods. For example, on All Saints' Day, children eat small cookies shaped like flat beans. They are called *fave dolce romane*, which means "sweet Roman beans."

Christmas in Italy is a time of religious worship and great festivities. Traditional activities include setting up nativity scenes to show the scene of Jesus' birth. Children enjoy visiting churches to see the beautiful displays. On Christmas Eve, people attend a midnight mass. As well, Christmas is a time

The roots of *Carnevale* lie in ancient festivals celebrated by the Romans and Egyptians, though Carnevale is now celebrated throughout Europe and the Americas and is the period that precedes the Christian season of Lent. This float parade *(left)* as well as masquerades, parties, dancing, and acrobatics are part of carnival festivities in Acireale, Sicily, which culminate on Shrove Tuesday, the day before the Lenten season begins. *Calendimaggio* (May Day) in Assisi *(above)* is one of the most important events of the year. Lasting for three days on the first Thursday, Friday, and Saturday in May, Calendimaggio celebrates spring and honors the memory of Saint Francis.

According to ancient pagan tradition known as the Devils' Dance, Easter morning is welcomed in the Sicilian village of Prizzi with devils running through the streets. People wear red-colored clothing, sheepskin, and wooden masks with horns and announce their presence by rattling chains around their wrists. These "devils" catch people and force them to offer something to drink. The dance ends only with the appearance of the statues of Jesus Christ and the Virgin Mary, which drive the devils out, symbolizing the eternal struggle between good and evil.

of holiday foods. Different regions of Italy have their own traditional Christmas dishes.

At Christmas, the legend of La Befana is often told, and children look forward to receiving gifts. In addition, they enjoy the custom of dressing like La Befana and visiting neighbors to beg for gifts. Common gifts, called *befanati*, are fruit and nuts. The legend of St. Nicholas, or Santa Claus, has made its way to Italy and may also be included in more traditional Christmas festivities.

Carnevale

During the six weeks before Lent, Italians enjoy a carnival, or *carnevale*, filled with music, dancing, costume parties, and food. For some carnivals, huge, fanciful floats in brilliant colors are built and paraded through the streets. For others, people don special costumes and march or dance in the streets. In the ten-day Venice Carnevale—dating as far back as 1268 when festivities lasted a month or more—costumed or masked people themselves parade

The Venetian Carnevale originated from a victory of the Repubblica della Serenissima (Venice) in a war against Virico in 1162. Wearing gaily colored costumes and acting in comedic performances that poked fun at social norms soon became a Venetian tradition. Since everyone was disguised, divisions between social classes blurred. The Venetian government supported this activity to encourage patriotism.

through the city's narrow streets and open squares. Along Venice's Grand Canal, there is a procession of gondolas, the long, narrow boats that carry people along the waterways. One of the largest carnivals is the Viareggio Carnevale, known for its impressive floats. Displayed on the floats are papier-mâché figures made to look like famous Italians—but instead of flattering, the likenesses are instead made to appear ugly! Children ride on the floats and toss candy into the lively crowds.

Family Traditions and Customs

Since most Italians are Roman Catholic, many family traditions revolve around Christian holidays. Ceremonies for baptisms, weddings, and funerals take place in churches. In addition to the religious celebration, however, families hold parties or feasts afterward where relatives and friends are welcomed to enjoy a meal with the family.

Weddings are huge, happy celebrations. In the Roman Catholic tradition, there is a formal ceremony in church followed by a lavish feast. The feast—with as many as fourteen courses—may be held outdoors, spread on tables covered in beautiful cloth. The bride and groom have a wedding cake and they toast each other with wine.

Long ago in the Roman Empire, girls often married as early as twelve years of age. Often times, the parents of the bride and groom arranged the marriage in advance. At the wedding, the bride wore white and was attended by a matron of honor. The couple said vows to one another and usually signed a contract of marriage.

In modern Italy, children also have their own special occasions. In Roman Catholic families, the most important celebration for children is receiving their first

Holy Communion. This special event takes place when the boy or girl is about eight years old.

Food and Wine Festivals

Food and wine festivals enjoy a long, rich history in Italy. This tradition of celebrating harvests dates back at least to the time of the Romans, who had many public holidays to give thanks to the gods. Many festivals marked important steps in the process of raising crops. For example, at the festival of *Fordicidia* on April 15, Romans sacrificed cattle. They believed this would help keep the soil fertile. Later, on June 9, they celebrated the festival of *Vestalia*, cleaning storehouses in expectation of the harvest.

In coastal towns in modern Italy, fishing festivals are also common. For example, the city of Taranto holds a festival at sea called the *San Cataldo*. People eat fried fish while watching a parade of passing boats. At other fishing festivals, fishermen form a procession through the streets along with children who push carts of fruits and vegetables.

Ancient Festivals and Traditions

Like much of Europe, Italy also suffered the ravages of the plague known as the Black Death during the Middle Ages, beginning first on the island of Sicily in 1347. July in Venice, however, is the traditional time to celebrate the end of the great plagues of Italy in 1576. In a symbolic "bridge of boats" Venetians place vessels side by side across a canal to reach the Church of the Redemption.

The Palio, an exciting bareback horse race, occurs every year in Siena, followed by a festival that continues for several days. On July 2 and August 16, people flock to the city's main square, Piazza del Campo, for

Italians in this photograph are celebrating Liberation Day. On April 25, 1945, the Nazi occupation of Italy ended, and the country was freed from twenty years of fascist dictatorship. Italians commemorate this national holiday with parades, parties, and ceremonies.

Crowds watch the Italian Republican Guard's military horses at the Palio. Every summer since the Middle Ages, the town of Siena holds the Palio, a bareback horse race reminiscent of the Middle Ages.

the race. Horsemen parade around in armor, and footmen march in elaborate medieval costumes. Flag-twirlers perform with brilliantly colored banners, called *palios*. Excited children sometimes run mock races on foot.

The race gets its name from a special silk palio decorated with a picture of Saint Catherine, Siena's patron saint, that the winner receives. Before the race, this banner is carried around the piazza in a wagon drawn by four white oxen.

Siena is divided into seventeen districts, and each district enters a horse and rider in one of the two races. Following tradition, the horses are selected by drawing lots, and then they are blessed in the local churches. The riders dress in the colors of their districts, often decorating the horses' reins and bridles. The race itself has no rules, and sportsmanship is not important. Participants may even use their riding crops to lash at other riders in an effort to get ahead. The winner is the first horse to cross the finish line after three laps around the track.

First recorded in 1283, the Palio may have originated in Roman military training. Other traditions say it grew out of ancient rivalries between regions of Italy.

THE RELIGIONS OF ITALY THROUGHOUT ITS HISTORY

6

When most people think about religion in Italy, they think of the Roman Catholic Church. From his headquarters in Vatican City, the Pope serves as chief religious leader for more than one billion Roman Catholics worldwide. According to the Catholic World News Web site, 97 percent of Italians were Catholic in the year 2000.

For nearly 2,000 years, Roman Catholicism, a religion founded on the life and teachings of Jesus Christ, has been active in Italy. At the heart of the Catholic faith is the belief that Jesus is the son of the one God. According to this faith, Jesus was sent to Earth and born to the Virgin Mary.

Many religious values of the Catholic faith are recorded in a group of writings called the New Testament. The twenty-seven sections of the New Testament, called books, tell the story of Jesus' birth, life, death, and resurrection from death. In addition, they record his teachings. Other books are letters written by early religious leaders. One example is the book called Romans, which is a letter written by Paul the Apostle to the Christians in Rome.

Holy Week, the most important religious festival in Italy, celebrates the resurrection of Jesus Christ. On Easter Sunday, spirited processions

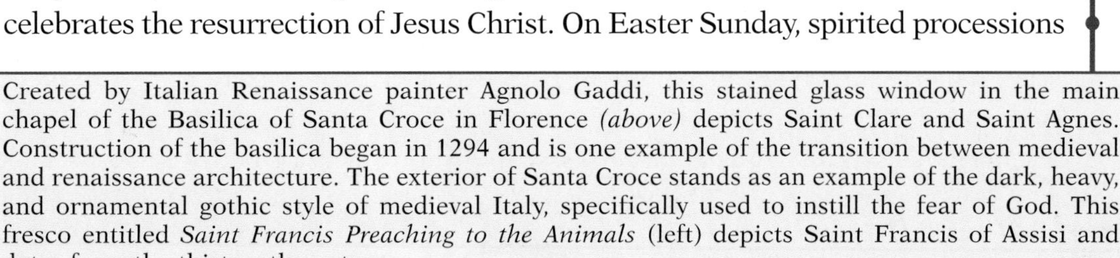

Created by Italian Renaissance painter Agnolo Gaddi, this stained glass window in the main chapel of the Basilica of Santa Croce in Florence *(above)* depicts Saint Clare and Saint Agnes. Construction of the basilica began in 1294 and is one example of the transition between medieval and renaissance architecture. The exterior of Santa Croce stands as an example of the dark, heavy, and ornamental gothic style of medieval Italy, specifically used to instill the fear of God. This fresco entitled *Saint Francis Preaching to the Animals* (left) depicts Saint Francis of Assisi and dates from the thirteenth century.

Pope John Paul II gives Christmas Mass at the Piazza San Pietro in Rome's Vatican City in 2002. He offered his *"Urbi et Orbi"* ("To the town and to the world") blessing, urging the world to avoid conflict in Iraq and appealing for peace between Israelis and Palestinians. The pope said that believers in all religions should build peace.

move through the streets. Marching bands, whose members dress in bright costumes, play joyful music.

From its arrival in Rome in the first century AD, the Catholic religion gradually grew stronger as it forced out pagan beliefs. It also eliminated the worship of Roman emperors, who were once given the status of god at death. Today, most Italians profess to be Catholics although Catholicism is no longer the state religion of Italy, and there is no compulsory religious education.

Monotheism in Rome

Before Roman Catholicism arrived in Italy, no single religion or god was held above the rest. The Roman Empire expanded across the map and included territories in the Middle East. In Jerusalem and other parts of Judea (modern-day Israel), a man named Jesus spoke out, claiming to be the son of the one true God. Jesus' closest followers were called disciples. According to the Bible, the disciple Judas Iscariot betrayed Jesus to Jewish

The Roman Forum

Romans gathered in city squares called forums to worship, shop, and conduct government meetings. The square at the center of the republic, called the Roman Forum today, marked the place where Rome was founded. Its ruins, uncovered in the nineteenth century, remind visitors of the activities that once took place there, including the worshiping of gods and goddesses in various temples. People came from all around the republic to meet in a building called a *curia*, including the Roman Senate. Others came to worship or shop. At the center of the Forum stood a golden milestone, from which all the roads of Rome began. On it were listed the distances to various parts of the republic. In fact, the popular saying "All roads lead to Rome" arose because the Romans built such an efficient system of highways that no matter which road one started a journey on, he or she would eventually arrive in Rome.

leaders in AD 33. They arrested him and persuaded Pontius Pilate, a Roman governor, to execute Jesus for breaking Jewish law.

Jesus' disciples continued to spread the teachings of the one God. According to Christian tradition, one of the disciples, Peter the Apostle, arrived in Rome to preach the teachings of Jesus. His message that there was one god, not many gods, angered some Romans. He was put to death on account of his faith, in AD 64. Around this same time, a terrible fire raged through Rome; Emperor Nero (AD 37–68) blamed the Christians. Afterward, this new religion continued to face huge obstacles in Rome.

But the teachings of Paul and other followers of Jesus continued to spread. A group of believers, called Christians, formed in Rome and gained converts. In response, the Roman Empire passed laws outlawing Christianity. Its belief in one god was in direct conflict with the belief in emperors-turned-gods and in other Roman gods. Many early Christians were persecuted for their beliefs. Others were arrested and put on trial. If they were found guilty, they were punished or put to death. It was during this same time that the practice of sending condemned Christians to their deaths in fights with wild animals in the Colosseum grew popular.

A History of the Catholic Church

Until the fourth century, the Roman Empire was generally hostile toward Christians. At this time, a few major changes occurred. Constantine (d. 337) became emperor in AD 306, and he converted to Christianity. He decreed that Christians—and all people—were to have religious freedom in the Roman Empire. Then, Constantine moved the capital of the empire from Rome to Byzantium (present-day Turkey). He named the new capital Constantinople, which then became the center of power in the empire, replacing Rome.

However, Rome continued to be the seat of power of the Catholic religion. The leaders of the Roman Catholic Church, called popes, still lived there. Constantine had given a parcel of land in Rome for the construction of a Catholic Church. Saint Peter's Basilica was built early in the fourth century, according to Catholic tradition, over the grave of Peter the Apostle. The roots of Roman Catholicism burrowed deep into the soil of Rome, making this city its home.

This illustration from the sixteenth century *(left)* shows Constantine the Great, founder of the Byzantine Empire and his empress mother, Helena. Helena helped found the Christian Empire of the Romans and was made a saint because of her charitable acts, including building churches in Rome and in the Holy Land. The Sistine Chapel *(right)* was built in the fifteenth century for Pope Sixtus IV. In 1508, Pope Julius II convinced Michelangelo Buonarroti to paint the chapel's ceiling. At the height of the Renaissance in 1512, Michelangelo completed the frescoes, which depict scenes from the lives of Moses and Christ.

Saint Peter's Basilica

Saint Peter's Basilica stands over a small *aedicula*—an underground shrine for a statue—called the Trophy of Gaius. Sections of the floor were removed to reveal an ancient Roman cemetery, discovered in 1939. According to Roman Catholic tradition, the shrine is also the burial place of Saint Peter. Early in the fourth century, the emperor Constantine ordered a church, called a *basilica*, built over the shrine in honor of the saint.

Over the next 1,200 years, the basilica gradually fell to ruins. In 1506, during the height of the Renaissance, Pope Julius II decided to rebuild this symbol of Christian faith. First, he ordered the ruins torn down. Then, upon reconsideration, he called together some of Italy's best artists to help design and rebuild it. The work took 170 years.

Some of the artists who worked on the basilica are Bramante, Michelangelo, Maderno, and Bernini. Donato Bramante (1444–1514) was the main architect, or designer, of the new church. Stefano Maderno (1576–1636) built the wide porchlike area, called a *portico*, at the dome's base. Bernini (1598–1680) created the glorious Throne of Saint Peter. He also built the colonnade, or pillar-lined walkway, that wraps around the open space in front of the basilica. Seen from above, Bernini's colonnade creates a space shaped much like a keyhole, with Saint Peter's Square inside. It is generally thought that Saint Peter's Basilica owes most of its grandeur to Michelangelo who took over the project in 1547 at the age of seventy-two, and also was responsible for the design of the dome.

For a time in the 1300s, however, it looked as though the Catholic Church would permanently move its base of power from Rome. During this time the popes chose to live in Avignon, France, and lead Catholics from afar. The Roman Empire in the West had fallen long ago, in the year AD 476. Now, with the departure of its Catholic leaders, Rome crumbled.

The election of Pope Martin V in 1417 brought important changes to the Catholic Church again. For a number of years before Martin V's election, there had been heated struggles for power within the church. Now, under the leadership of Martin V, the church grew more stable and its leaders could refocus their energies. During the mid-1400s, the popes turned their attention to the old seat of the church, to Rome, with an eye toward rebuilding the forgotten city.

At this time, the Renaissance was sweeping through Italy. Some of the greatest artists of the day helped to refurbish Rome. Next to Saint Peter's Basilica, the Sistine Chapel was built for Pope Sixtus IV. Michelangelo di Lodovico Buonarroti Simoni (1475–1564) painted the ceiling and west wall of this little chapel, decorating them with scenes from the Bible. Modern tourists from around the world are drawn to Italy each year to see Michelangelo's beautiful work.

Other Renaissance artists created works for particular popes or for churches, chapels, and monasteries. Raffaello Sanzio (1483–1520), commonly known as Raphael, painted *Madonna Sistina* for Pope Julius II. In the Santa Maria delle Grazie, a monastery in Milan, Leonardo da Vinci (1452–1519) created the magnificent fresco *The Last Supper*. For the cathedral in Florence, Filippo Brunelleschi (1377–1446) designed the dome. Lorenzo Ghiberti (1378–1455) sculpted splendid bronze doors for the cathedral's baptistery. Well into the sixteenth century, the popes of Rome were dedicated to beautifying and building churches and works of art.

These plaques memorialize Casullo Mario Varzi and Deglialberti Guido Varzi, two teenage brothers who died with their siblings at Mauthausen, a Nazi concentration work camp located in Austria, which operated during World War II. The plaques are part of an Italian memorial at Mauthausen.

Basilica of Saint Francis of Assisi

After Francis of Assisi (AD 1182–1226), a poet and nature lover, was declared a saint in 1228, a church and monastery were built in his honor. Saint Francis was the first known Christian to experience stigmata (spontaneous wounds on the hands and feet corresponding with Jesus' wounds from his crucifixion). Saint Francis also experienced visions of Jesus and the Virgin Mary. In 1210, he founded an order of friars now known as Franciscans.

Sometimes called San Francesco, the basilica stands in the medieval town of Assisi, Italy, where Francis was born. Artists such as Pisano, Giovanni Cimabue, Giotto, Pietro Cavallini, among others, have illustrated the story of Saint Francis's life. In 1818, the remains of Saint Francis were moved to a crypt beneath the church.

On September 26, 1997, a huge earthquake rocked the hills of Umbria and the town of Assisi. The vividly tinted frescoes in the Basilica, like the detail shown above, cracked into tens of thousands of fragments, crashing to the floor of the church and scattering in dusty pieces. Later, more pieces rained down on friars who had gathered to examine the damage. With care, they collected the tiny pieces for reconstruction. In September 2002, Giotto di Bondone's (1267–1337) restored thirteenth-century fresco of St. Jerome (also known as *The Doctors of the Church*) was unveiled to the wonder and relief of the townspeople of Assisi. Though it is no longer complete, the restored masterpiece has restored the hope of the people of Assisi.

Leonardo da Vinci's masterpiece *The Last Supper*, painted between 1495 and 1497, was one of the most popular and influential works of the Renaissance. Shortly after the painting's completion, it gained a prestigious reputation as a masterpiece. However, da Vinci's experimental use of tempera on plaster was technically unsound, and by 1500 the painting had begun to deteriorate. Since 1726, several restoration attempts have been made, most recently in 1976.

During the Renaissance, the Papal States were located in the regions of modern Lazio, Umbria, Marche, and part of Emilia-Romagna. Their boundaries were protected with the help of military troops from countries whose rulers supported Roman Catholicism.

After the Kingdom of Italy formed in 1861, the papal territories of Emilia, Umbria, and Marche voted to join it. Then, when France pulled out of the kingdom in 1870, the Italians took Rome against the wishes of the pope, and made it the kingdom's capital. Living in the Vatican, the popes in Rome called themselves "prisoners" and refused to accept Italy's authority over their territory.

Finally in 1929, under the Lateran Treaty, Italy gave the territory of Vatican City to the Catholic Church. The borders of the Vatican were finally set. Today Vatican City is walled completely, except for an area in front of Saint Peter's Square.

The Shroud of Turin

First discovered in a church in fourteenth-century Constantinople (present-day Istanbul) Turkey, the Shroud of Turin is believed by Christians to be the image of Jesus Christ after his body was crucified in AD 33 and wrapped in linen. Claimed by Pope John Paul II to be the "true, real, and substantial presence of Christ," the Shroud has undergone a series of scientific tests to determine its age. In 1988, carbon-14 dating validated its age to the Middle Ages (estimates ranged from 1260–1390), but later studies claimed that past treatments—including one that removed grime with vegetable oil—had corrupted the study. Other recent analysis traced its date to the eighth century. Now residing in the Cathedral of San Giovanni in Turin, Italy, the Shroud remains one of the most compelling and mysterious symbols of Christianity.

Other Religions

Although the vast majority of Italians are Catholics, the country also has small numbers of Protestants, Jews, and Muslims. The Italian constitution guarantees the freedom of religious practice, but relationships between religious groups and the government are arranged by leaders from each group. For example, in 2002, the government signed agreements with Jehovah's Witnesses and Buddhists. They received the same legal rights as those given to Catholics. Muslims, on the other hand, have not worked out an agreement with the Italian government. As a result, Italian law may not protect Islamic religious practices, such as those having to do with marriage or burial.

Jews date the practice of their faith in Italy to the Middle Ages. Although the Jewish population in Italy is small, approximately seventy-five Jewish synagogues have been built around the country.

When Benito Mussolini befriended Adolf Hitler in the 1930s, he mimicked Hitler's attitude toward the Jews and passed anti-Jewish laws beginning in 1938. When Germany occupied Italy during World War II, Hitler ordered the capture of

Saint Padre Pio

The famous Italian priest, Padre Pio (1887–1968), was made a saint on June 16, 2002 in a canonization ceremony given by Pope John Paul II. Though the decision was made posthumously, thousands of Christians celebrated in his honor in and around St. Peter's Square in Rome for Sunday mass. Known during his life as a miracle-worker, healer, and mystic, witnesses claim that Pio suffered since 1918 from reccurring stigmata, or inexplainable bleeding wounds that often appear on the hands and feet. Christians believe that because the bleeding of stigmata resembles the wounds that were inflicted upon Jesus Christ, that this is a sign directly linked to God. Padre Pio is beloved all over Italy and throughout the Christian world as one of its greatest saints.

Jews and sent them to death camps. However, many Italians refused to obey these laws. Secretly they helped Jews hide from soldiers and escape to safer countries. Today, Jews in Italy enjoy religious freedom alongside people of other faiths. On January 27, 2001, Holocaust Memorial Day was established as a day when countries around the world could remember Holocaust victims. Italy has joined Germany, Poland, Israel, and others to observe this day. In January 2002, Italy aired a documentary on Giorgio Perlasca, an Italian who helped save more than 5,000 Jews.

Immigrant Muslims from Morocco, Albania, Tunisia, Senegal, and Egypt have brought the Islamic religion to Italy. In addition, some native Italians have converted to Islam. In all, there are an estimated 719,000 Muslims currently living in Italy.

Muslims have built many small places of worship, mostly in Italy's northern regions. With financial support from foreign nations, three large mosques have been built since 1980. In eastern Sicily, Italy's first large mosque opened in the city of Catania, financed in part by the Libyans. Eight years later in Milan, the Al Rahaman Mosque opened. In 1995, after twenty years of construction, Rome's first mosque was completed. The structure, paid for mainly by Saudi Arabia, has been called the largest mosque in Europe.

THE ART AND ARCHITECTURE OF ITALY

7

Some of the world's most magnificent works of architecture can be found in Italy. From cathedrals and theaters to aqueducts and walls, Italian structures illustrate a long history of artisanship. Some of the amphitheaters, statues, and aqueducts built in Roman times still stand, a testament to the remarkable skill of Roman engineering. In fact, the abundance of art and architecture in Italy's public places creates the sense that the country itself is a living museum.

Roman Architecture

The Romans borrowed many of their building ideas from the Greeks, but soon Roman invention blossomed with its own identity. The Romans invented a new way to construct walls by using bricks and mortar. They reinvented the way buildings were designed using the shape of an arch. With its natural ability to support weight, the arch soon became common in Roman doors and windows. On a grander scale, arches supported soaring ceilings and roofs. Outdoors, arches formed the support system for bridges and aqueducts. The use of bricks and mortar, much lighter in weight than marble, allowed the Romans to engineer structures with several levels.

In 1751, Italian architect Nicola Salvi completed the Trevi Fountain in Rome *(left)*, which displays the sea god, Neptune, on a chariot pulled by horses. Legend has it that if you toss a coin over your shoulder, you will someday return to the "Eternal City." In the Italian town of Sulmona, ancient aqueducts *(above)* once transported water to Rome's central piazza. Romans built eleven major aqueducts in ancient Rome between 312 BC and AD 226. These aqueducts supplied the city with twelve million liters of water per day, which was used for drinking, baths, gardens, and fountains.

The Roman Colosseum was the first permanent amphitheater built in Rome and held blood sport events such as gladiator fights. Below the wooden arena floor was a complex set of rooms and passageways. The Colosseum also possessed elevators to raise and lower animals between floors.

One of the most famous multilevel structures showing Roman arches is the Colosseum. Built in Rome, its construction began in the first century, perhaps in AD 70. An outdoor stadium, this huge structure covers 6 acres (2.4 hectares) and could seat as many as 50,000 people. In the arena at its center, gladiators once clashed in hand-to-hand combat and men fought vicious animals to the death. Even women and children were subject to the brutal slayings, which were often inflicted as capital punishments. Directly under the elliptical arena floor was a complex system of rooms and passageways. It was here that prisoners and animals waited until they were hoisted from the lower level onto the wooden arena floor.

Later, during the Middle Ages, the Colosseum fell into ruins and continued to collapse because of earthquakes, lightning, and vandals. For centuries it stood silent. Then in the 1990s, the great stadium was restored. By 2000, plays were performed in the arena, filling the grand stadium with life after 1,500 years of disuse.

The freestanding Colosseum was unlike earlier Roman theaters that were built into natural hollows. In these earlier theaters, the rings of marble seats for spectators were set firmly on supporting earth. At the lowest level, a small stage formed the center. Some of these theaters were designed so well that an actor's onstage whispers carried all the way to the highest rows of listeners. In-ground theaters surviving in Italy include the Greek Theater in Sicily and the Arena in Verona.

The Romanesque Period

The Roman era was followed by a period known as the Early Christian or Byzantine period in Italian architecture. In parts of Italy that were influenced by Byzantium, the art of mosaic was resplendent. One of the most important examples of this kind of architecture is Saint Mark's Basilica in Venice, which shimmers with gold. During the Romanesque period (1050–1200), there was a revival of buildings whose size and structure resembled those of the Roman Empire. In Pisa, a city in Tuscany, the Leaning Tower stands as a famous work of medieval architecture. Begun in AD 1173, it was designed as part of a group of monuments, including a cathedral, baptistery, and cemetery. Even before construction was finished, the bell tower began settling into the soft ground at its base. Bonanno Pisano, the engineer in charge, tried to make up for the tower leaning to one side. He made the top three of the eight stories taller on one side than on the other side. However, his plan backfired. The extra weight on that side caused the tower to sink further.

By the late twentieth century, the tower leaned about 15 feet (4.5 meters) to the side. If the pattern of sinking continued, it could collapse. Finally, modern architects removed some earth from beneath its foundation between 1990 and 2001. Although it did not stand perfectly upright, the tower now leans about 17 inches (44 centimeters) less than it had before. The architects predict that it will take approximately 300 years for it to sink again to the dangerous tilt it achieved in 1990.

During the Middle Ages, Gothic architecture marked by domes, pointed arches, turrets, and pinnacles became popular. The Duomo in Milan, for example, one of Italy's best-known

The Leaning Tower of Pisa has survived for more than eight hundred years. Construction began in 1173. The architect is unknown, but the original benefactor was a wealthy widow named Bertha. Construction stopped when money was redirected to fight a war; however, the Pisans continued construction in 1350. Originally built to boast Pisa's wealth, especially toward neighboring Florentines, the city and its remarkable bell tower were eventually sold to Florence in 1392.

Construction on the Florence Cathedral began in 1296 under the direction of Arnolfo di Cambio and took nearly 150 years to complete. The magnificent dome for which the cathedral is famous was designed and built by Filippo Brunelleschi in 1436.

Gothic cathedrals, has more than 3,000 statues built onto its outer walls. The cathedral itself is gigantic—the third-largest church in Europe—with interior room for more than 20,000 people. Its construction, begun in 1386, continued for 500 years.

The Renaissance

The period known as the Renaissance remains the most famous time of artistic development in Italy. The word "renaissance," meaning "rebirth," refers to the years that followed the Middle Ages, from about 1400 to 1550. During this time, artists and writers studied classical Roman and Greek art, architecture, and literature. The rebirth of these arts touched all areas of life in Italy. In time, the Renaissance movement spread across all of Europe.

Three artists in particular were major influences on the work of practically all Renaissance artists. Donatello (1386–1466), a Florentine sculptor, carved the marble statue *St. George* around 1415. The sculpture is remarkable for showing the human form as powerful, functional, and confident in personality. Filippo Brunelleschi (1377–1446), an architect, designed the dome for Florence's Santa Maria del Fiore cathedral in 1419. With this work, he bridged the way from Gothic to Renaissance architectural techniques. Around 1427, Masaccio (also called Tommaso di Giovanni di Simone Guidi; 1401–1428), painted the frescoes of the Brancacci Chapel in Florence's Church of Santa Maria del Carmine. His new technique of using color and light added depth to painted figures.

Leonardo da Vinci, another Florentine, painted some of the most celebrated works of the Renaissance era. Portraits such as the *Mona Lisa* earned the admiration of fellow artists and established him as a master. On da Vinci's canvases and wooden panels,

Leonardo da Vinci painted his famous portrait *Mona Lisa* circa 1503 to 1505. This was da Vinci's most beloved portrait, and he carried it wherever he traveled. The painting has long been admired for the enigmatic smile of Mona Lisa, who is believed to be the wife of Francesco del Giocondo.

people and objects took on a new perspective. Before da Vinci, figures had appeared flat and without dimension. His religious paintings, including *The Last Supper*, which depicts Jesus sharing a meal with his disciples before his crucifixion, often showcase warm, glowing hues.

Da Vinci's genius, however, was not limited to painting. His notebooks, journals, and other projects show his brilliance as a scientist, sculptor, mathematician, architect, inventor, and writer. He has been called the first "Renaissance man," a term for a person who is skilled in many different areas.

From the Tuscany region came Michelangelo, another celebrated Renaissance artist. Michelangelo was a brilliant sculptor, architect, painter, and poet. His statue *David*, which stands more than 14 feet (4.25 meters) high, is considered one of the greatest works of all time. Sculpted during 1501–1504, the statue presents a visual image of Renaissance values: the beauty, dignity, and nobility of mankind.

Michelangelo also created frescoes in the Sistine Chapel. Working on this project for more than eleven years lying on his back atop huge scaffolding, he painstakingly re-created scenes from the

Michelangelo Buonarroti, an influential Renaissance artist, created this sculpture, *Pietà*, in 1498. The *Pietà*, which means pity, details the Madonna holding Christ after he was crucified.

Pope Julius II commissioned Raphael, circa 1506, to decorate the Vatican with frescoes, which are created by applying paint to a moist plaster surface. The most notable of these paintings is *The School of Athens*, which glorifies philosophers Plato, Aristotle, and Socrates, and the mathematicians and scientists Euclid, Pythagoras, and Epicurus in one fantastical portrait.

Bible. These images, now famous the world over, each have their own names, including *The Last Judgment* and *Creation of Adam*.

Other famous works by Michelangelo include tombs for the Medici family, the Laurentian Library, and the *Pietà* (sculpted twice—the first for Florence's cathedral and another for the pope).

A great many more artists created amazing works during this time including Raphael, known for his frescoes such as *The School of Athens*; Sandro Botticelli (1445–1510), who painted portraits and frescoes such as the *Birth of Venus*; and sculptor Lorenzo Ghiberti, who sculpted *The Sacrifice of Isaac*.

Baroque and Neoclassical Styles

The architectural style that followed the Renaissance in Italy is called Baroque. Baroque is synonymous with Rome and its two great architects of the period—Gian

Gothic architecture, such as the Milan Cathedral pictured in this photograph, developed in England and France during the twelfth century. Gothic architecture is a highly ornate and elaborate style, which is distinguished by large stained-glass windows, gargoyles, tall skyscraper-like towers, and arched windows and doors. These structures were built to inspire people to think of God when they looked up at their overwhelming features.

Lorenzo Bernini (1598–1680) and Francesco Borromini (1599–1667).

Bernini, whose patron was Pope Urban VIII, completely transformed the face of Rome with his palaces, piazzas, and fountains such as the Fontana dei Quattro Fiumi in Piazza Navona. Bernini's great rival was Borromini who designed buildings with complex geometry, such as the Chiesa di Sant' Ivo alla Sapienza in Rome.

During the eighteenth century, a brief spell of creative architecture flourished. Known as neoclassical, this period is exemplified by structures such as Rome's Scalinata Spagna, or Spanish Steps, and the Trevi Fountain. Considered the world's most famous fountain, the Fontana di Trevi is a spectacular display of water and sculpture. The focal point is Neptune, god of the sea, driving his chariot through the waters. The flow of water, delivered by ancient Roman aqueducts, comes from 14 miles (22.4 km) away. Built over a span of thirty years beginning in 1732, the fountain was ordered by Pope Clement XII. Niccolò Salvi (1697–1751) and Pietro Bracci (1700–1773) are its artists.

Modern Art and Design

Italy's modern-day artisans create handicrafts according to centuries-old traditions. One such place where old-world craftsmanship continues is the city of Florence. Tiny shops line narrow streets where craftsmen create beautiful leather goods, hand-colored papers, woodcarvings, jewelry, and metal sculptures. Many of the businesses were once guilds where young people learned skills from master artists. One famous spot in Florence is the Ponte Vecchio, where goldsmiths' shops line the sides of the city's oldest bridge.

Since the thirteenth century, glassmakers in Venice have produced various types of glass. *Cristallo*, or crystal, is a clear glass perfected during the fifteenth century.

Constructed in 1345, Florence's oldest surviving bridge, the Ponte Vecchio (Old Bridge), stretches across the Arno River and contains small craft shops along its sides and top. Between 1565 and 1800, an upper level and a back level of shops were added, which ultimately increased trade. During the Middle Ages, Cosimo de Medici ordered the removal of the original shopkeepers of butchers, tanners, and blacksmiths, who used the river below as sewage disposal, and replaced them with goldsmiths and artists.

Other popular Italian techniques include ways of coloring glass, gilding it, or enameling it. One very old technique bonds together strips of different colors of glass. When cut, the glass shows small bead or flower-like shapes. North of Venice on the island of Murano, glassblowers are famous for their chandeliers, vases, and other glassware.

In the regions of Umbria, Tuscany, and Sicily, majolica ceramics are handcrafted. This tradition dates back to the fourteenth century, when ceramics made by Spanish Moors (Muslims) were shipped from Majorca to Italy. Clay is shaped into platters, vases, mugs, bowls, and other shapes. Next, each item is glazed, then painted in vivid hues. Then it is glazed again and fired in a kiln. Some of the pieces are unique, such as pitchers shaped like roosters' heads.

In Cremona, a town in northern Italy, some of the world's finest violins, cellos, and violas are constructed. Perhaps the best-known craftsman of violins is Antonio Stradivari (1644–1737). The Latin form of his name, Stradivarius, was engraved on the instruments he made during his long career. Today, one of those prized pieces can receive between $500,000 and $1.5 million dollars at auction. Modern Italian artisans

On Stradivarius violins, the label, whether genuine or fraudulent, reads "Antonius Stradivarius Cremonensis Faciebat Anno," indicating the maker, where it was made, and the year of construction. However, thousands of violins were made later as inexpensive copies of seventeenth- and eighteenth-century originals. Affixing a label with the master's name was not done to be deceptive but rather to indicate the model from which it was designed.

make violins in the tradition established by Stradivari. Each one requires seventy to eighty pieces of wood, including maple, spruce, and at least five other types. Once the wood is cut and glued, it dries and cures for a year. Then, thirty coats or more of varnish finish its gleaming surface.

Other handicrafts stock open-air markets and stores in cities across Italy. Leather goods include bags, belts, and shoes. Tourists and locals alike are attracted to alabaster sculptures, wood carvings, and handmade lace. Others are drawn to rugs, handmade paper, or beautiful embroidery.

Italy's folk art is closely tied to its festivals and to the legends of its past. For example, for religious festivals and processions, participants create images of saints or symbolic arrangements of flowers. Children and adults enjoy the tradition of wearing special costumes for festivals and processions.

Also popular in Italy's folk art are subjects from myth and literature. Roman and Greek gods and goddesses as well as characters from great works of literature have inspired folk paintings and puppet shows. For example, in Sicily a popular figure is Orlando. Several Italians have written great works about Orlando's adventures. Among these writers is the Renaissance poet Ludovico Ariosto (1474–1533), who wrote *Orlando Furioso*. Orlando's adventures inspire Sicilian paintings and puppet shows. One of the stories of Orlando describes his unreturned love for Angelica, which drives him *furioso*, or mad.

To this day, Italian art and architecture are appreciated throughout the world. Modern Italian designers in the fashion, publishing, film, graphic, and industrial design industries continue to take their place among the world's most well-respected artists.

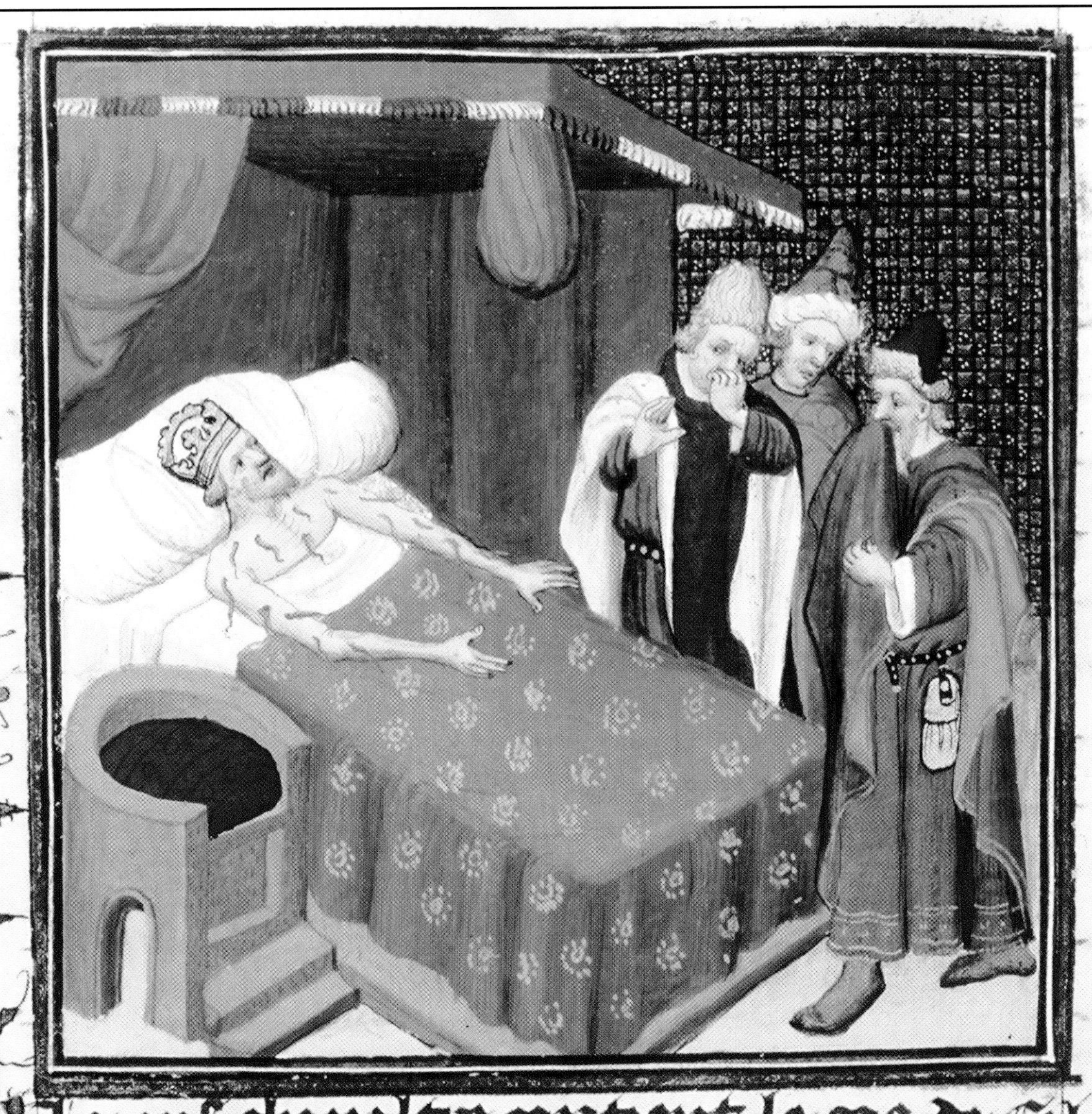

le. ix.e chapitre contient le cas de Gallerius surnomme maximian empere
des rommains et commence ou latin.
Gallerius em Gallenus. &c.
pereur de romme plein de pu-
lenteur et de pourriture et de

THE LITERATURE AND MUSIC OF ITALY

8

Virgil's *Aeneid*. Dante's *Inferno*. Umberto Eco's *The Name of the Rose*. Italian literature, both ancient and modern, has fascinated and delighted readers the world over. The earliest written works were poems, plays, histories, and speeches. Novels and short stories came later, along with written versions of traditional folktales. Italy has always contributed its share of thoughtful writers to the world stage. During the twentieth century, six Italian writers were honored with Nobel Prizes for literature, including Giosuè Carducci (1906), Salvatore Quasimodo (1959), and Eugenio Montale (1975), each for their poetry, and Grazia Deledda (1926), Luigi Pirandello (1934), and Dario Fo (1997) for drama and/or fiction.

Roman Literature

Rome's history of great literature traces its beginnings to the life of a slave. Livius Andronicus, a Greek laborer, was born around 284 BC in what is today Taranto, Italy. After he was freed from slavery, he lived in Rome and taught Latin and Greek. He translated the *Odyssey*, written by the Greek poet Homer, into Latin, calling it *Odusia*. This was the first major poem in Latin. In 240 BC, he produced the first dramatic performance in Rome during a festival called the *Ludi Romani*. After this, he wrote and staged a number of tragedies and comedies. Only a few fragments of his written works survive.

A French drawing *(left)*, created in 1350, illustrated Italian novelist Giovanni Boccaccio's book *The Decameron* and depicts the use of leeches as a curative measure for the bubonic plague. During the fourteenth century, the use of leeches as well as chopping up a snake every day and sleeping on the left side of the bed were all thought to be effective treatments against the bubonic plague. Niccolò Machiavelli (1469–1527), Italian political theorist and writer *(above)*, began his career as a politician in Florence. However, after the collapse of the republic he was forced into retirement. The book *The Prince* for which he is most famous, was published posthumously and in 1559 was on Pope Paul IV's list of prohibited books.

Grazia Deledda (1871–1936), an Italian novelist, won the Nobel Prize in literature in 1926. She is best known for her stories of Sardinian peasantry and depictions of the life and customs of the small Sardinian village of Nuoro, her lifelong home.

Of Italy's ancient writers, the most famous is probably Virgil (70–19 BC). The well-educated son of a successful farmer, Virgil joined the court circle of Emperor Augustus. Here he received the support of the imperial minister Maecenas (d. 8 BC), a patron (sponsor) of the arts. Virgil is best known for his epic poem, *The Aeneid*, begun around 29 BC. Twelve volumes long, it was still unfinished at the time of his death. The poem tells the legend of the founding of Rome by Aeneas of Troy. Important characters in the poem are Greek heroes as well as

Roman Writers

Livius Andronicus (284–204 BC) Translated Homer's *Odyssey* into Latin. Produced Rome's first publicly performed play.

Cicero (106–43 BC) Wrote brilliant speeches on politics and law. Founded the method of writing and speaking called Ciceronian rhetoric.

Virgil (70–19 BC) Wrote *The Aeneid*, a long poem about the legendary founding of Rome.

Horace (65–8 BC) Wrote, among other things, short lyric poems in stanzas of two or four lines—now called the Horatian ode.

Livy (c. 59 BC–AD 17) One of the greatest Roman historians.

Seneca (4 BC–AD 65) Roman politician and lawyer, skilled in writing on moral issues; also skilled in writing tragedies. The Senecan tragedy influenced Shakespeare and other Renaissance writers.

This engraving of Italian poet and professor of literary history, Giosuè Carducci (1835–1907), appeared on the cover of the Italian magazine *L'Illustrazione Italiana* on July 17, 1892. Carducci won the Nobel Prize in literature in 1906. He was a highly influential literary figure and was regarded as the unofficial poet of modern Italy. His poetry modeled the Roman and Greek classics.

Greek and Roman gods. The *Aeneid* also describes Emperor Augustus's work to unify and stabilize the Roman Empire.

Virgil is often called Italy's greatest poet, although others believe Dante's works rival Virgil's works. Virgil's great skill was recognized in his own time. For example, a Roman mosaic shows Virgil seated between two muses—the epic Muse and the tragic Muse.

Much of what we know of Rome's early history comes from writers such as Livy and Julius Caesar. Livy (c. 59 BC to AD 17) recorded Rome's history by focusing on people and events, as well as politics. And instead of writing in Greek, as earlier historians had done, he wrote in Latin. Another writer of history was Julius Caesar, dictator of Rome from 46–44 BC. Caesar wrote about the Gallic War and the Roman civil war.

Medieval Writers

Often called Italy's greatest poet, Dante Alighieri wrote *The Divine Comedy* between 1308 and 1321. This three-volume work is made up of the *Inferno* (Hell), *Purgatorio* (Purgatory), and *Paradiso* (Paradise). Most well known is the *Inferno*, which describes the poet's journey through the nine circles, or layers, of hell. Along the way, he points out particular people who are being punished at each level. At the bottom and worst level of hell, Satan is frozen in ice. *The Divine Comedy* was the first major work to be written in Italian, the common language, instead of Latin.

During the time Dante was writing, Giovanni Boccaccio (1313–1375) wrote *The Decameron*, a collection of 100 stories. The poet Francesco Petrarch (1304–1374) developed the form of the sonnet, a style of poetry, now called the Petrarchan sonnet

This photograph, taken in 1919 of Luigi Pirandello (1867–1936), Italian novelist and dramatist, appeared in the Italian magazine *L'Illustrazione Italiana*. Pirandello won the Nobel Prize in literature in 1934. His first widely acclaimed novel, *The Late Mattia*, was published in 1904. In 1916, he turned his attention to theater and found this career shift profitable and successful. Pirandello excelled at playwriting, turning out as many as nine plays a year, most of which were successes. Between 1922 and 1924, he became a major public figure throughout Italy, Europe, and America. He is hailed as the greatest Italian playwright of his time.

(in contrast to the Shakespearean sonnet). One of Petrarch's most memorable subjects is a beautiful woman named Laura, whom he loved from afar. The image of Laura, with her blond hair and white skin, is one of the great images of Italian poetry. In the 1500s, Niccolò Machiavelli (1469–1527) wrote *The Prince*, a book of advice on how to gain and keep political power. Baldassare Castiglione (1478–1529) wrote a book of a different kind of advice. In *The Book of the Courtier*, Castiglione offered suggestions on how to dress and behave well in court.

Modern Writers

In more recent times, Italy's greatest contribution to modern literature has been in the forms of the novel and short story. Italian writers such as Luigi Pirandello (1867–1936) and Umberto Eco (b. 1932) have won international praise. Born in Sicily, Pirandello enjoyed a long career writing plays, novels, and short stories, including *Six Characters in Search of an Author*. Pirandello, who died in Rome, won the Nobel Prize for literature in 1934. Umberto Eco is a university professor of communication in Bologna, Italy. In part, his great reputation rests on his studies of signs and symbols in language. In addition, his 1980 mystery novel *The Name of the Rose* became a worldwide best-seller. A film based on the book, starring Sean Connery and Christian Slater, was released in 1986.

Among other modern Italian authors of note is Italo Calvino (1923–1985). Born in Cuba, Calvino immigrated to Italy while still young. He was a journalist, novelist, and short-story writer. He is best known for his fables and fantastic tales, including *The Nonexistent Knight* and *The Baron in the Trees*. He died in Siena.

An outstanding female novelist and playwright is Dacia Maraini (b. 1936). Her works include *Dialogo di una Prostituta con su Cliente* (Conversation Between a Prostitute and Her Client) has been performed internationally by her female theater company.

Folktales

Italy's literature includes stories written especially for children. One of the earliest writers to record traditional folktales and fairy tales was Giambattista Basile. Born around 1575 in Naples, Basile worked as a soldier and public official. During his career, he collected folktales and fairy tales and wrote them down in his own style. Afterwards, he created a "frame story" to hold all the tales together. In Basile's story,

Italian author Carlo Collodi is best known as the creator of Pinocchio. The first chapter of *Pinocchio* appeared in 1881 and was an immediate success. However, church fathers feared it would encourage rebellion since critics felt *Pinocchio* had an antiauthoritarian tone because of the contrast between wealth and poverty and the negativity about the judicial system. This color lithograph is the cover of a 1935 edition.

This 1690 portrait of Antonio Stradivari (1644–1737) shows the famous Italian violin maker at his workbench. His interpretations of geometry and design of the violin have served as models for violin makers for more than two hundred years. Stradivari also made harps, guitars, violas, and cellos, a total of 1,100 instruments of which 650 survive today.

ten women tell fifty stories to a prince and his wife over the span of five days. Characters in the tales include Puss in Boots, Rapunzel, Beauty and the Beast, and Cinderella.

Basile was one of the first authors to write down these tales, which until that time had been passed down by word of mouth. His collection of stories inspired fairy-tale writers in other countries, including the Grimm brothers in Germany and Charles Perrault in France.

In 1881, Carlo Collodi published *Pinocchio*, the tale of a wooden puppet who becomes a real boy. The story first appeared in the *Giornale dei Bambini* (Children's Magazine). Later, it was published as a storybook and translated into many other languages.

Italian Music and Opera

Italy is the birthplace of various types of music, including operatic singing, and musical instruments such as the piano. For example, an early form of singing is the Gregorian chant. Named after Saint Gregory I (pope from 590 to 604), the chant was used during mass in the Roman Catholic churches.

The Catholic Church was also the setting for the musical advances of Guido D'arezzo (990–1050), a monk. In the early eleventh century, Guido made improvements to the system by which music is written down. At the time, a two-line system was used (the lines for F and C). To these, Guido added a line above the C and another between the C and the F. In this way, pitch could be noted. Also, Guido changed the way of writing musical notes. Instead of using the letters *a* to *p*, as was common, he created a system using only letters *a* to *g*. These letters could be used in combinations of capital letters, small letters, and double small letters to show notes. Guido's system is the standard Western method of writing down music today.

This photograph shows Giacomo Puccini (1858–1924) seated at the piano in the room at his house in Torre del Lago, where his operas came to life. Puccini descended from musicians and is considered the most important Italian opera composer after Verdi. He began his career at age fourteen as an organist for a local church. With a scholarship and financial support, he continued his musical endeavors at Milan Conservatory. His first opera, *Manon Lescaut*, achieved considerable success. Puccini wrote twelve operas during his life, and as a perfectionist, revised all of them even after they opened.

During the Renaissance, the rebirth of art included a new enthusiasm for music and song. Composers experimented with new ways to write music, while artisans crafted violins, cellos, harpsichords, and other instruments. In cultured society, a well-educated person was expected to play an instrument, if not several. In ballrooms, the psaltery (an ancient stringed instrument) and the *lira da braccio* (an ancestor of the violin) were popular. The lira da braccio was a stringed instrument much like a fiddle. The lute, an instrument whose strings are plucked, was popular with the rich as well as with peasants.

The word "opera" comes from the Italian phrase *opera in musica*, which means "work in music." Until the Renaissance, Italy's plays were usually religious in theme and were performed by actors who spoke their lines. Then, music composers began experimenting by setting plays to music. Instead of speaking their lines, the actors began singing them, and opera was born. Playwrights experimented with themes, too, and wrote plays with

Giuseppe Verdi

Giuseppe Verdi (1813–1901) made his well-received debut with *Oberto conte di San Bonifacio*, produced at La Scala in 1839. But when audience members rudely rejected his next opera, he suffered deeply. Despite this setback, Verdi grew to become Italy's leading opera composer, with works produced internationally.

Literature was often Verdi's muse. During the 1840s, he composed works inspired by the writings of Victor Hugo, Lord Byron, Voltaire, and others. One of his strongest operas from this period is *Macbeth*, inspired by Shakespeare's play. Later he wrote *Otello* and *Falstaff*, based on Shakespeare's *Othello* and *The Merry Wives of Windsor*. Produced at La Scala in 1893, *Falstaff* was Verdi's last dramatic work. Its enthusiastic reception was an ironic contrast to the hissing that had greeted *Un giorno di regno* (King for a Day) a half century earlier.

Verdi is best remembered for operas such as *La Traviata* (The Fallen Woman; 1853), *Rigoletto* (1851), and *Aida* (1871). He helped move opera style from one that placed highest importance on the singers' voices to one that placed equal importance on the voices and the drama of the plot. For this reason, Verdi's operas are some of the most memorable of all time.

secular (nonreligious) themes. As opera spread around the world, non-Italian composers often used Italian, the language of the original operas. Early on, Milan became known as the center of opera in Italy.

La Scala (Teatro alla Scala), in Milan, is one of the most famous opera houses. It was built to replace the Royal Ducal Theatre, which burned down in early 1776.

Luciano Pavarotti sings as Cavaradossi from the Italian opera *Tosca*. The Italian tenor made his debut to the singing world in 1961 when he won the international Achille Peri prize at the age of twenty-six.

After the fire, owners of the opera boxes at the Royal Ducal provided funds to build a new theater on land occupied by the Church of Santa Maria alla Scala. It was from this church that the new opera house received its name. The first performance in La Scala, on August 3, 1778, was Antonio Salieri's *L'Europa riconosciuta*.

Some of Italy's most celebrated opera composers lived during the nineteenth century. Giuseppe Verdi (1813–1901) is remembered for *Don Carlos*, *La Traviata*, and *Rigoletto*, among many other operas. Amilcare Ponchielli (1834–1886) is noted for *La Gioconda* (The Joyful Girl). Giacomo Puccini (1858–1924) is best known for *La Bohème*, *Tosca*, and *Madama Butterfly*.

In recent years, ancient Roman ruins have been used as the backdrop for many operas. For example, a large amphitheater in Verona, as well as the Baths of Caracalla in Rome, have provided a magnificent stage for operatic performances.

Renowned modern opera singers include Luciano Pavarotti and Andrea Bocelli. Pavarotti, born in 1935 in Modena, Italy, is known for his ability to sing flawlessly the highest notes of a tenor's range. Some of his best-known operatic roles are the duke in *Rigoletto*, Tonio in *La Fille du Régiment*, and Radamès in *Aida*.

An opera singer of a different sort, Bocelli rose to fame in the 1990s because of his concert performances and recordings. His 1997 album, *Romanza*, has sold more than fifteen million copies. Blind since the age of twelve, he is unable to perform most stage roles in operatic productions. Despite the challenge, he has sung arias in *The Merry Widow* and performed the title role in *Werther* at the Detroit Opera House. He was nominated in 1999 for a Grammy Award and an Oscar. However, some critics who prefer that opera singers remain faithful to classical styles have faulted Bocelli's sound for being too "pop," playfully calling some of his works "popera."

CARNE
ant.
al kg. L.700

FAMOUS FOODS AND RECIPES OF ITALY

9

Italy's pasta, flavorful soups, sauces and cheeses, as well as its crusty breads are a delight to people around the world. Dishes that began as regional specialties, such as in Tuscany, have been added to menus by chefs worldwide.

A typical Italian meal begins with antipasto, usually a selection of cold meats. Afterward is pasta or rice, followed by a main course of meat, fish, or fowl. Salad is served after the main course, and a little fruit and cheese usually finishes the meal.

Of all foods, Italy's pastas are perhaps its most famous. Common types are spaghetti, linguini, *maccheroni* (macaroni), and fettuccini, among others. Spaghetti is an easily prepared favorite. Italians enjoy it with sauce, topping it in dozens of ways. *Spaghetti con salsa alla Bolognese* is spaghetti with meat and tomato sauce. More unique is *spaghetti al sugo di pesce*, or spaghetti with fish sauce. Fettuccini, thin noodles made of wheat and egg, is often served with a sauce of meat or tomato, or with chicken livers or pecorino (a hard, strong-tasting cheese). Lasagna, a wide flat noodle, is layered with meats

Before an Italian family (above) begins to eat they say "Buon appetito!" which means "Enjoy your meal!" Pasta is served at many Italian meals and young children learning how to twirl the long noodles around their fork use a large spoon to keep the pasta in place. There are many different kinds of pasta served other than spaghetti, and most have amusing names to describe their size and shape: *agnolotti* means fat little lambs, *orecchiette* means little ears, and *farfalle* means butterflies. Fresh chicken, sausages, and meats *(left)* are available at Italian meat markets. Meat products are one of the most important agricultural products in Italy.

The man pictured here is presenting one of the most popular dishes in central Italy, *spaghetti alla chitarra*. Made from fresh pasta, the dough is pressed through a rectangular loom device called a *chitarra* (guitar), where it falls gently onto a wooden board in fine strands of spaghetti. It can be cooked immediately for the aforementioned dish, or carefully dried and used within a few days for another meal.

and cheeses. Ravioli, small pasta pockets, are filled with tasty mixtures of spinach and cheese, such as ricotta.

In Italy, soups are also popular. There are fish stews, mussel soups, and pasta-based soups. One popular soup is minestrone, a meat-free soup of vegetables and pasta. Often minestrone soup is eaten during Lent, a time when many people abstain from eating meat. *Brodetto*, a traditional soup, is usually made during the Easter holiday and consists of beef or lamb broth, egg yolks, cheese, stale bread, and spices. Christmas fare includes *cappelletti in brodo*, a soup made of a long list of ingredients, including beef and chicken broths, meat-stuffed ravioli, cheese, and spices.

Regional Fare

Regions of Italy are each known for their own specialty dishes and cooking styles. For example, Lombardy is known for its risotto (rice cooked in broth), polenta (baked cornmeal porridge), and panettone (a light cake made with dried fruit), among other foods. Sicily is known for its fried seafood. The Piedmonte region uses lots of garlic and other spices as well as

Merchants in Milan sell a variety of cheeses, such as mozzarella, ricotta, and provolone. Renowned twentieth-century Italian fiction writer Italo Calvino is quoted as saying, "Behind every cheese there is a pasture of a different green under a different sky." This is because the taste, aroma, and nutrient composition of cheese is directly affected by how cows and sheep are raised.

Fresh Tomato and Italian Sausage Pizza

The earliest pizzas, made by the Neapolitans (people of Naples), were plain crusts topped with tomato and garlic. The unsalted crust in this recipe is in the traditional style. Nowadays, pizza toppings are limited only by the chef's imagination!

- 1 pkg. dry yeast (1/4 oz or 7 g)
- very warm water (from the tap is fine)
- 3 cups (0.72 l) all-purpose flour
- 8 oz (0.23 kg) spicy or sweet Italian sausage
- 6 or 7 medium-sized Roma (plum) tomatoes (the egg-shaped kind)
- 3/4 lb (0.34 kg) sliced (or grated) mozzarella
- 1 tbsp (15 ml) chopped Italian (flat-leaf) parsley
- 2 or 3 tbsp (30–45 ml) olive oil, plus extra for cooking/baking

Preheat oven to 425°F (218°C).

Mix Dough: In small bowl, dissolve yeast in ½ cup (120 ml) warm water. Set aside. Measure flour into large bowl. Add yeast mixture. Stir, adding ¼ cup (60–120 ml) warm water to make a soft dough. Flour hands and knead dough several minutes until smooth. Cover with clean towel to avoid drafts and set aside.

Prepare Toppings: Cook sausage over medium heat until browned, with a little olive oil if needed. When it has completely cooled, crumble it into small pieces. Set aside. Wash and core tomatoes. Slice each in half lengthwise, then lay it on the flat side. Cut in thin slices. Set aside.

Build Pizza: Flour hands and punch down dough. Drizzle a few drops of olive oil over 13–15-inch (32.5–37.5 cm) pizza pan and spread evenly. Next, spread dough into pan, pushing and stretching it to edges. Lay cheese slices (or grated cheese) on dough. Next, arrange tomato slices in circular pattern over cheese. Add crumbled sausage. Sprinkle chopped parsley on top. Finally, drizzle with olive oil and rub oil into edges of crust.

Bake It: Bake on middle rack in oven for about 25 minutes, until edge of crust is lightly browned.

many types of meat and fowl—roasts, veal, venison, partridges, and pheasants. In contrast, Tuscan cuisine is simple and elegant, centering on the use of olive oil, subtle spices, and good wine. Liguria produces an excellent *pesto*, an oil-based sauce containing basil, garlic, cheese, and pine nuts.

Italy produces a wide variety of cheeses, from the strong, tasting provolone to the soft, creamy ricotta. In Piedmonte, two popular local cheeses are Robiola, made from sheep's milk, and the smooth, milky Fontina d'Asti. In Lombardy, cheese makers excel at producing gorgonzola (blue-veined and sharp-tasting) and mascarpone (cream cheese). Frequently found atop pizzas are mozzarella and *parmigiano* (parmesan). A tasty snack, *mozzarella alla Milanese* is breaded slices of cheese, deep-fried.

Italian desserts run the gamut from gelato (a soft ice cream) to cannoli (pastry tubes filled with sweetened cheese). Pistachio nuts are popular additions to sweets in Sicily (*gelato al pistacchio*, for example), while chestnuts coated in sugar or chocolate

Ancient Roman Sweet Treat

This recipe is from an ancient recipe book by a Roman named Marcus Gavius Apicius. He called this treat *Aliter Dulcia* (Another Kind of Dessert). It makes a crumbly, nutty, sweet snack best eaten with a spoon!

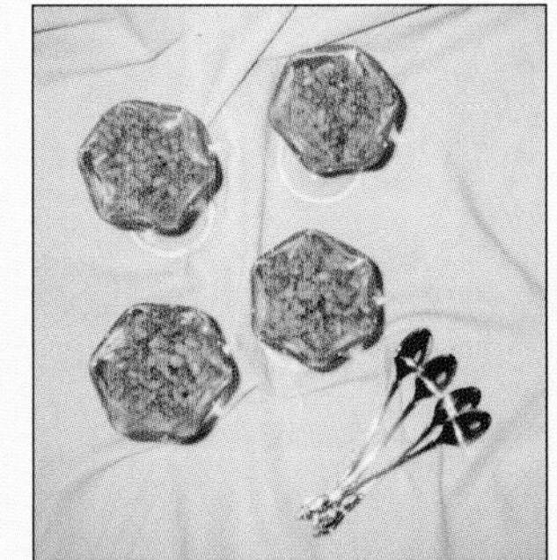

8 oz (226 g) chopped walnuts and/or almonds
4 oz (114 g) pine nuts
1/4 cup (63 ml) honey, plus more for drizzling
1/4 cup (63 ml) grape jelly (Romans used *passum*, a sweet sauce made from grape juice)
1/4 cup (63 ml) milk
2 eggs
Ground pepper to taste

Mix together all ingredients except pepper. Place mixture in medium-sized saucepan. Cook on stovetop over medium heat, stirring frequently, until mixture thickens, or about five minutes. Cool slightly, spoon into small serving dishes. Drizzle with honey and sprinkle with pepper to taste.

are popular elsewhere. Spumoni is ice cream layered in different flavors. All sorts of cakes, tarts, and pies are served on holidays, special occasions such as weddings, or simply as a treat to enjoy with family or friends.

At Easter, Italians enjoy a traditional pie called *La Pastiera*. Its crust holds sweetened ricotta cheese, candied citrus fruit, essences of vanilla and orange, and other ingredients. Many families have their own recipes for this Easter pie. Other Easter treats include cakes shaped like lambs, chocolate cherry cookies, and chocolate eggs with toys inside.

A tour of Italian tastes is not complete without a sampling of beverages. Served in tiny cups, Italian espresso is a very strong coffee. Another coffee drink, cappuccino, is espresso mixed with boiling foamed milk. Wine accompanies most lunches and dinners, and even children may drink a little with their meals.

Gelato is the Italian word for ice cream, but that's where the similarity ends. Gelato has less sugar and fat than ice cream does, and less air, which gives it a rich, creamy texture. The ancient Romans had a version of gelato literally called "frozen pleasure," which combined pureed fruit with honey and snow. The current version of gelato was invented by the Chinese, who taught the Arabs, who taught the Sicilians, who are now considered the best gelato makers in the world. It wasn't until the 1500s that Sicilians used hand-cranked machines—and not snow—to make the frozen dessert.

DAILY LIFE AND CUSTOMS IN ITALY

10

While all natives of Italy consider themselves Italian, their cultural identity is generally linked more tightly to their region than to Italy as a whole. Each region has its own unique history, festivals, dialect, foods, and customs. In Italian, the word for this loyalty to a specific region is *regionalismo*. Northern regions of Italy include Piedmonte, Valle d'Aosta, Liguria, Lombardy, Trentino-Alto Adige, Friuli-Venezia Giulia, Veneto, Emilia-Romagna. The central regions are Tuscany, Latium, Umbria, and Marche. Italy's southern regions include Abruzzi, Molise, Campania, Basilicata, Puglia, and Calabria. There are also the islands of Sicily and Sardinia.

Urban Life

City life in Italy can be crowded and noisy. For example, Rome is known for its terrible traffic flow and is home to more than one million automobiles and motor scooters. Traffic noise is normally so loud that it can cause a gradual loss of hearing. During peak times, the traffic creeps along so slowly that often a person can walk faster than the automobiles are traveling. For this reason, motor scooters have

Rome *(left)*, the capital of Italy and seat of the pope, has expanded well beyond the ancient boundaries of the city as they were established by Emperor Aurelian in the third century. The design of the ancient city has been preserved, however, and is considered modern, even by today's urban planners. Ancient marble columns and ruins stand alongside apartments and noisy boulevards. Rome continues to be the center of transportation, accessible by rail, road, and sea as well as serving a cultural and religious importance internationally. Rome's economy depends largely on tourism, such as the man *(above)* enjoying Italy's café lifestyle in this contemporary photograph.

A young boy plays with his mother and grandmother in Saint Mark's Piazza in Venice. More than 70 percent of Italy's population lives in urban areas. Many working parents rely on grandparents to look after their children. There is no national child-care system in Italy and only 7 percent of parents use private day-care services.

become a popular alternative to cars and buses in many Italian cities.

But urban life is not only about traffic and noise. Nearer the edges of smaller towns and suburbs people usually live in larger, private homes. However, most city inhabitants live in small apartments with balconies, where they grow plants, talk with friends, or play board games. A popular game with young people is *reversi*, played on a board with thirty-two squares. Though more complicated than tic-tac-toe, the object of the game is similar.

No matter where families reside, they enjoy gathering to visit and talk in the central squares, called *piazzas*. All small towns have a piazza, and cities may have several. Here, people gather to relax, visit with friends, take a stroll, or simply enjoy the sunshine.

Rural Life

In rural areas, the crowds of the cities give way to spacious stretches of fields,

Men chat on a busy street during the Palio festival. Visits to family and friends are an important part of the Italian lifestyle. In Italy, an evening or Sunday afternoon stroll is a well-established tradition. On weekends, many Italians go to the beach or countryside, or to sporting events.

An elderly farmer rakes leaves on a farm in the Po River Valley. Wheat, maize, and barley are the major crops grown in Italy. Olives and citrus crops are also common, which, together with vineyards, make the country an agricultural leader throughout the Mediterranean and Europe.

rolling hills, and mountain slopes. Most agricultural communities are in southern Italy and on the islands of Sicily and Sardinia. In northern Italy, the Po River Valley is a fertile farming area. Farms are typically family-run, producing wheat, maize, and vegetables. Livestock include sheep, swine, oxen, water buffalo, goats, and horses.

Despite the space and beauty of the countryside, southern agricultural families face daunting hardships. Over the centuries, deforestation has caused soil and land quality to grow poor. Unreliable rainfall and the difficulty of farming on mountainsides are additional obstacles. Since most of the nation's wealth is concentrated in the cities, rural regions may lack paved roads, electric power, schools, and proper housing. Over the past few decades the government has been working to improve these conditions. Nevertheless, the hardships have driven many to immigrate to other parts of the country or even out of the country—to the Americas or other countries in Europe.

In old Italy, large families were commonplace. Today, the birthrate for every woman of childbearing age is approximately 1.2 births. This means that the population is experiencing a period of slower growth. Children still have a special place in Italian society, however. Parents include their children in most social events and allow them to stay up late to play in the piazza while they and the grandparents enjoy a drink in a nearby café.

La Famiglia

Regionalismo is important to Italians, but even more important is *la famiglia*—family. Traditionally, extended families have lived quite close to one another. Frequently relatives gather to enjoy meals, social activities, and outings. The younger generation looks out for and often cares for their aging parents. Although this is a tradition that is slowly changing, most young Italians tend to live with their parents until they get married. Children are valued members within the extended families, as are older parents of grown children who take care of their grandchildren while parents work. Daycare centers are uncommon except in Italy's largest cities.

Household sizes in Italy have been getting smaller over the past several decades. In 1961, the average household size was 3.6 people—this means most households had three or four people. By 2000, the average size had shrunk to only two or three people. In part, Italy's population size is falling because women are having fewer children now than they had in the past. In 2000, the average Italian family had only one child. Currently, in Italy, there are more deaths than there are births, a trend that is shrinking its population. According to the Italian National Statistical Institute, Italy's population will likely drop by about 6.5 million people by the year 2050.

Italian Pastimes

Italians' everyday life involves many of the same pastimes common in other European and American homes. One of the most enduring pastimes of the Italians is the evening

During the 1998 World Cup playoffs, Italian Fabio Cannavaro competed against French player Zinedine Zidane. Italy lost this game to France, who won the cup in the final round against Brazil. The World Cup championship games are held every four years since they first began in 1930. Today, soccer has become one of the most internationally popular games with 140 countries competing and more than one billion fans.

stroll, or the *passeggiata*. Members of a family, couples, or friends usually take short walks before dinner, greeting one another and catching up with news in the community or daily happenings and events. The passeggiata is a way for entire neighborhoods to keep in close touch with each other.

Across most of the country, a large draw for Italians of all ages is sporting events and competitions. Soccer is among the favorite athletic activities for Italians, who call it *calcio*. Introduced in the 1800s, calcio became truly popular in the 1930s and has now become such a way of life for most Italians that the country's regions are often in stiff competition with one another. Many Italians spend Sunday afternoons watching their favorite teams in calcio matches on television. Extending beyond what others might feel is typical sportsmanship, many Italians are so passionately involved with the game that they may rush the field of winning players or loudly berate a losing team.

Boccie is a game that originated in ancient Rome during the battles of Rome's Punic War against Carthage, which started in 264 BC. Teams were composed of two, four, six, or eight men, and soldiers threw a small stone called a "leader." Next, larger stones would be thrown at the "leader" and the stone coming the closest scored. Boccie continued to be played until 1319 when Holy Roman Emperor Charles IV prohibited it because he thought it interfered with sports of military nature. The ban was lifted years later when the medical faculty at Montpelier, France, declared boccie the best exercise to prevent rheumatism.

That was the exact case in 1986 when a group of fans arrived at an airport to criticize their team's failure to bring home the World Cup. Italian soccer players have positioned Italy among the top three World Cup teams. In all-time World Cup rankings, Italy places third, after Brazil and Germany. Italy has won the World Cup in soccer three times, in 1934, 1938, and 1982 and has hosted the World Cup tournament twice, in 1934 and 1990.

Sports fans and athletes enjoy a wide variety of other activities, too. On Italy's coasts, sailing, swimming, and skin diving appeal to natives and tourists alike. Others enjoy fishing, boat racing, and waterskiing. Just as well liked are cycling, car racing, horse racing, tennis, volleyball, golf, hiking, and hunting. Making its way from America, basketball has also gained popularity in Italy. As a result, American players sometimes sign contracts to play for Italian teams.

An Italian style of lawn bowling called *boccie* (sometimes spelled *bocce*) is popular, especially in Piedmonte and Liguria.

The most popular cycling event in Italy is the Giro d'Italia, where cyclists trek 1,709 miles (2,750 km) of Alpine terrain, including many of the steepest roads in Italy. On May 14, 2002, Italian cyclist Mario Cipollini won the third stage of this event, which is the 128-mile (206-km) stretch.

Played on a long, narrow clay or sand court, the game focuses on rolling balls. The object is to get a ball closest to the target ball (called the *pallino*) and to knock away the opponents' balls. In the United States, Australia, and South America, Italian communities have picked up the sport as well.

The slopes of the Alps are a popular setting for winter sports. Skiing, snowboarding, and skating are a few common activities. In 1956, the Winter Olympics were held in Cortina d'Ampezzo. In 2006, Italy will again host the Winter Olympics, this time in Turin.

In ancient Rome, enthusiastic crowds cheered on chariot races. Today, bicycle races and automobile races provide a similar thrill. During races, spectators line the roads to see the athletes pass. Each May during the *Giro d'Italia* (Tour of Italy), cyclists ride the length of Italy, from a southern city such as Leece to a city in the north, usually Milan. If the race starts in a city on the island of Sicily, a special break is scheduled for the cyclists to transfer to the mainland to continue to race. Scheduled in stages, the race is twenty-five days long. Not just for Italian cyclists, the Giro d'Italia draws athletes from around the world.

As with bicycle races, spectators gather along Italy's highways to watch automobile races. Famous worldwide, the *Mille Miglia* (Thousand Miles) takes racers along 1,000 miles (1,609 kilometers) of highway. In May 2002, the husband-wife team of Giuliano Canè and Lucia Galliani won, driving a BMW 328. Serious crashes during the 1939 and 1957 races killed spectators and, in the latter year, two drivers as well. Although the race was discontinued after each crash, it later made a comeback.

Watching television is also an overwhelmingly popular activity in Italy. Listening to the radio is quite common as well. In addition, Italians enjoy going to the movies. At more than 4,900 cinemas in Italy, moviegoers in 1999 purchased a total of more than 100 million tickets.

EDUCATION AND WORK IN ITALY

Italy's school year runs from September to mid-June. For Italian students, a typical school day begins at 8:30 AM and ends around 12:30 or 1:30 PM. At this time, students go home for lunch, and the official school day is over. During the afternoon, children work on homework and may play sports. The school week is six days long, with Sundays off.

Education

Italy's school system is divided into six levels. The first three levels—kindergarten through lower secondary (middle) school—are required by law. In this system, most youngsters are in school between the ages of six and fourteen or fifteen. In addition, many attend nursery school at three or four years of age and stay in school past age fifteen.

Most children attend public schools. Here, they study and learn in class sizes of nine to thirteen students, on average. In class, students learn from schoolbooks and other books written for young readers. In 2000, more than 6,200 textbooks were published in Italy. Besides learning from printed materials, students may learn from

A large group of Catholic schoolchildren *(left)* arrive on the island neighborhood of Giudecca for the Feast of the Redeemer, crossing the Giudecca Canal from the main islands of Venice. This is a pilgrimage that Venetians make on the third Sunday in July to honor the Virgin Mary. A manuscript illumination from the fifteenth century *(above)* is titled *A Lecturer at the University of Bologna*. The University of Bologna began as a law school and is the oldest surviving institution of higher learning in Italy. The earliest Italian universities were established in the ninth century and began as scholastic guilds.

computer software programs or from the Internet. In 2000, only 15 percent of households had access to the Internet, although that number is growing rapidly each year. In contrast, more than 85 percent of schools used the Internet in 2000, according to the Italian National Statistical Institute.

At some schools, students have additional outlets to pursue interests in the arts, theater, or sports. Most public schools have sports facilities of some sort. Around half offer artistic workshops, and perhaps a third offer theatrical workshops.

Maria Montessori

In the early twentieth century, Maria Montessori's teaching methods changed the face of childhood education. At the *Casa dei Bambini* (Children's House), Montessori (1870–1952) set up a school that did not require students to sit in desks to learn. Instead, they had the freedom to learn from activities and materials that worked best for their learning styles.

Using the Montessori method, teachers provide materials that appeal to the natural curiosity and interests of each child. Beads strung in graduated-number groups teach early math skills. Specially designed wooden slabs prepare young eyes for left-to-right reading patterns. Sandpaper-coated shapes of letters and numbers encourage little fingers to explore and think about the alphabet, counting, and math. Children work and learn at their own paces, while teachers are nearby but not center stage.

Nowadays, Montessori schools are established throughout the world. Many of Dr. Montessori's writings remain in print, including *The Montessori Method*, first published in 1912.

Sicilian schoolchildren in grades one through three learn together in their shared classroom at the San Giovanni School. Italian students are required to attend school for eight years. The maximum class size is twenty-five students, and the curriculum includes Italian, foreign languages, mathematics, science, geography, social studies, religious history, art, music, and physical education.

A small number of Italian children attend private schools. In lower secondary school, around 5 or 6 percent of students attend Catholic schools. That number is much higher at the kindergarten level (41 percent).

At around age fifteen, students take an exam to exit lower secondary school. It is usually about this time that they and their parents make choices about the kind of future for which to prepare. Teenagers who want to continue their education go on to upper secondary school. Depending on their interests, they may choose a college preparatory school or *liceo*, a teacher-training school or *magistrale*, or a vocational institute focused on industry, agriculture, or commerce. Depending on the type of study, this stage of schooling may last from three to five years. For example, a vocational program may require three years, while college-prep programs require five years. Whatever their chosen course, students are required to work hard.

Most teenagers—about 84 percent in 1999—choose to go to upper secondary school. Some young people, however, choose to become apprentices in a particular trade or craft instead. An apprentice gets hands-on training by working as an assistant to an experienced tradesperson. For example, one teenager may apprentice himself to a jeweler, while another assists a glassblower or leather worker.

Upon completion of upper secondary school, students take a national exam. This difficult exam has written and oral (spoken) portions. By the time a student takes this exam, he or she has reached the age of nineteen. With a diploma, a graduate may apply for admission to a university.

Italian universities offer programs in many fields of study, including science, law, teaching, psychology, architecture, medicine, chemistry, and others. In the academic year beginning in 1999, the programs that attracted the most new students were law, economics and statistics, and engineering.

Work in Italy

Jobs in Italy are in great demand by college graduates and other trained professionals. Women and young people have a higher rate of unemployment than do men. Knowing that work is often difficult to find, many university students extend their studies longer than the usual five years required to earn a degree. By prolonging graduation, they delay the prospect of unemployment. Many

In Sora, Italy, a worker makes paper in a Fabocart paper mill factory. Traditional Italian workdays are Monday through Friday, 8 AM to 1 PM and 3 PM to 7 PM, but the American nine-to-five routine is starting to spread throughout the north. Italy's economy is the fifth largest in the world, overtaking the United Kingdom in 1987. The Italian economy is based on agriculture in the south and industry in the north.

Italians in their twenties who have not found work live at home with their families and help out in the household.

The largest job sector in Italy is the services industry, which employs about 13 million Italians, while only one million people work in the field of agriculture. In 2000, about 6.8 million people worked in industry (including metalworking, construction, mining, textiles, food, wood, and energy).

In terms of income and education, the northern regions of Italy fare better than those in the south. The country's industry and trade are based in the north, generating more jobs and better pay for northerners. Forming a busy triangle, the cities of Milan, Turin, and Genoa are at the center of Italian industry. Milan is home to the Italian stock exchange and most of the nation's international banks.

In contrast, workers in the southern regions must rely on agricultural jobs that offer low wages. Unemployment is worse in the south. According to the Central Intelligence Agency's (CIA) *World Factbook*, more than 20 percent of southern Italians were unemployed in 2000, compared to a national rate of 10.4 percent. The plight of the Mezzogiorno, or southern part of Italy, troubles many young Italians. In the south, one manner of expressing opinions about "the southern problem" is through *posse*, a kind of political rap music that rose to popularity during the late 1980s.

The Mafia

The Mafia, or secret criminal society, has long affected Italian industry. During the late Middle Ages, the first *mafie*—small private armies—simply protected lands in Sicily for absent landholders. Soon, however, they made themselves the sole law of the land. By 1900, Mafia bosses led "families" who controlled sections of Sicily, including the financial system (economy). They enforced their control with whatever means were necessary. Violence was common, whether in power struggles or in acts to avenge family honor. The Mafia system spread to Italy's mainland.

Over time, the Mafia became so powerful that it was a huge force in Italy. Increasingly, it became involved in illegal drug trafficking and other criminal activities. Members demanded protection money from people and murdered those who did not cooperate. Organized crime families lead by bosses battled one another. The Mafia spread to other countries, including the United States.

The Mafioso, members of organized crime, have been linked to government leaders and other prominent people. With the support of Italians old and young

An engineer works on a Ferrari engine at the factory in Maranello. Industry in northern Italy is centered on the Industrial Triangle of Turin, Milan, and the port of Genoa. Industry developed in this area because the flat land was ideal for building large factories. Also, the reliable roads and the port at Genoa make it easy to export the finished goods.

alike, Italy's government is working to rid the nation of the Mafia, though it has been notoriously difficult to eliminate.

Made in Italy

Among products made by Italian workers, the most recognized worldwide are probably clothing, leather goods, and automobiles. Headquartered in Milan, the fashion industry boasts some of the greatest designers in the world and attracts some of the most extravagant buyers. Giorgio Armani, headquartered in Milan, is known for his smart, comfortable fashion for businesspeople and his namesake perfume, *Giorgio*.

Known for fashionable bags, belts, and shoes, Guccio Gucci began his business in 1921 in Florence. By 1938, he had opened a shop in Rome. A Gucci store opened in New York in 1953, the year of the designer's death. Today, Gucci stores are located around the world, with the largest on Fifth Avenue in New York City.

This Fiat is parked on the street in Rome. Fiat, an acronym for *Fabbrica Italiana Automobili Torino*, began in 1889 and is one of the oldest European automobile companies. Today, Fiat is renowned for making exceptional, practical vehicles and has a monopoly on car manufacturing in Italy, controlling 90 percent of the market. However, in 2000, Fiat merged with General Motors to compete with the newer car manufacturers.

Other fashionable Italian labels in clothing, furs, and shoes are Valentino, Versace, Dolce & Gabbana, Fendi, and Ferragamo—just to name a few.

From the flashy Ferrari to the practical Fiat, Italian automobiles are known around the world. At the racetrack, Ferraris have taken thousands of drivers to victory since 1947, the year Enzo Ferrari first introduced the Italian car. Ferraris made for the road instead of the racetrack are just as coveted, even though prices range from about $200,000. Whatever the intended use, Ferraris are known for their elegance, beauty, and speed. Other Italian luxury cars are the Alfa Romeo, Lamborghini, Maserati, and Lancia. Less spectacular, but no less important, is the little Fiat, a car designed for the everyday driver.

Italian director Federico Fellini (*right*) stands in front of the poster for *La Dolce Vita* (The Sweet Life) with the film's star, Marcello Mastroianni. The film explores the life of a gossipy newspaper columnist who becomes involved in the lives of the elite Roman society of the 1960s. Fellini's film won a Best Foreign Film Oscar and the Palme d'Or, or "Golden Palm" award at the Cannes Film Festival.

This photograph of Roberto Rossellini and Ingrid Bergman was taken on location in Rome during the filming of *Europa 51*. Rossellini is considered one of the greatest directors of Italian film. He received international fame in 1946 for his film *Open City* which was secretly made in Italy during the Fascist period. He is best remembered for his low budget, shaky camera work, and stories dealing with life in a country stricken by war.

Living in one of the most popular tourist destinations of the world, most Italians find that tourism touches their everyday lives. In fact, Italy ranks fourth in the world as far as income from international tourism is concerned.

The Film Industry

Cinecittà (Cinema City), just outside Rome, is similar to Hollywood in the United States. Here, directors and actors come together with a myriad of other workers to make movies.

Italy's film industry began more than a century ago, when the first commercial film was made in 1896. In the early twentieth century, filmmakers faced strong competition from American and British companies, who found sunny Italy ideal for film locations. In the 1930s, however, Mussolini drove out foreign film companies. He established a national cinema institute and restricted what Italian filmmakers could put in their works. After World War II, restrictions relaxed, allowing more freedom and

A restoration expert uses a computer to find likely matches between some 120,000 fragments of Florentine painter Cimabue's priceless thirteenth-century portrait of Saint Matthew and a photograph of the masterpiece. The fresco of Saint Matthew was destroyed in an earthquake, which occurred on September 26, 1997, and toppled the ceiling of the Basilica of Saint Francis of Assisi, where the painting was housed.

creativity in film. The period from the 1950s to the 1970s saw the emergence of talented, internationally renowned Italian directors. One of the most important directors was Federico Fellini (1920–1993), whose greatest international hit was *La Dolce Vita*. More recent directors include Guiseppe Tornatore whose *Cinema Paradiso* (Cinema Heaven) won an Oscar in 1990. Other important directors include Roberto Rossellini, Vittorio De Sica, Luchino Visconti, and Bernado Bertolucci. Italy has also produced a number of extremely famous actors. The most well-known Italian actors are perhaps Marcello Mastroianni and Sophia Loren, who was honored in 1991 in Hollywood with an Academy Award for her lifetime achievement in film.

Italy's Future

As Italy looks toward its future, topics such as reform are high priorities. Among the most pressing problems are organized crime (especially the Mafia), illegal immigration, high unemployment, and poverty in its southern regions. In areas of money and politics, Italy has participated in the ongoing unification of European countries. Italy is a member of NATO and the European Union (EU). In January 2002 the euro replaced the lira as the country's official currency.

As citizens of a democratic republic, Italians—even teenagers—may take part in setting the course of the country. Women were granted the right to vote at the end of World War II, casting their ballots for the first time in the election of 1946. Today, at age eighteen, all citizens of Italy have the right to vote.

ITALY

AT A GLANCE

HISTORY

The earliest known settlers of current-day Italy were of Indo-European origin. This means they migrated from the areas of central Europe and southern Russia. Arriving around 4000 BC, these ancient peoples divided into twelve tribes by around 2000 BC. Some of them were the Ligurians, Veneti, Italics, and Sicles. Around this time, the Terramare came from central Europe, settling the Po River Valley. Also attracted to this area were the Villanova, a group of unknown origin. Then, starting around 1200 BC, Phoenicians from the Middle East joined the mix of peoples, primarily on Sicily and the southern mainland. Around the same time, the Etruscans settled the northern mainland. Finally, between 700 and 600 BC, Greeks began settling southern Italy and Sicily where the Phoenicians had been. The area became known as Magna Grecia (Greater Greece).

According to legend, Romulus and Remus, twin sons of Mars, the god of war, founded Rome in 753 BC. More likely, Rome sprang from groups of farmers and shepherds in that same area. With the rise of Roman power, the territories of Italy were unified as the Roman Republic in 509 BC. The republic became the Roman Empire, dominating the Western world until the AD 400s. Following the fall of the empire, the territories were repeatedly invaded, captured, and lost by various powers. The Roman Catholic popes controlled portions of central Italy around Rome.

Between 1500 and 1861, rulers from Spain, Austria, and France held power in Italy. However, beginning during the Renaissance, Italians gradually moved toward a sense of national identity. A slow movement toward unification arose, leading to the reunification of Italy in the 1860s and the withdrawal of French forces. Clinging to their power, the popes refused to yield Rome. But in 1870—against the wishes of the popes—the papal territories were finally incorporated into Italy. From 1870 until 1922, the Kingdom of Italy was a constitutional monarchy with an elected parliament. After Mussolini's fascist reign, during the 1920s and through World War II, the Republic of Italy was founded in 1946. Thus unified and organized, Italy has functioned under this government since then.

ECONOMY

Since World War II (1939–1945), when the Italian economy was completely devastated, Italy has evolved from an economy based mainly on agriculture to one based on industry. In fact, in the year 2002, Italy ranked as the world's fifth-largest industrial nation. Producing a similar amount of industrial output are France and the United Kingdom. Italy belongs to a group of eight industrialized nations that together are called the Group of Eight (G-8).

Although Italy ranks as a productive industrial nation, it is truthfully the northern regions that are most industrial. The southern regions remain tied to agriculture, mainly through family-run farms and olive groves. This division between the north and the south creates a sharp economic contrast. The standard of living is lower in the south, and unemployment rates are higher.

Italy's economy depends on a combination of imports and exports. For example, since much of the land is unsuitable for food production, the nation imports a good deal of foodstuffs. As well, natural resources are few—mainly fish and natural gas. Therefore, Italy imports more than 80 percent of its energy sources. The country is especially adept at importing raw materials, producing from them a steady supply of manufactured goods. Typically, manufacturing takes place in small- and medium-sized family-owned firms. Automobiles, clothing, and leather goods are but a few of these products.

After the terrorist attacks on the United States on September 11, 2001, Italy's economy has slowed down. A slow economy means that little buying and selling takes place. Italy was not alone in this change, for many countries—especially those in the European Union—saw similar results in their economies. However, by mid-2002, Italy's economy had begun to recover.

Italy has focused on a couple of main goals for its economy moving into the twenty-first century: lowering the nation's massive external debt and keeping inflation in check. Due to wage adjustments, monetary policies, and cutbacks in government spending, Italy is making progress with these goals. Italians have reason to be optimistic about their country's economic future.

GOVERNMENT AND POLITICS

Italy has been a democratic republic since June 2, 1946. The chief government leaders are the president, who is elected to a seven-year term, and the prime minister, who is appointed by the president and approved by Parliament. In May of 1999, President Carlo Azeglio Ciampi took office. In June 2001, Silvio Berlusconi was appointed prime minister.

Italy's current constitution took effect on January 1, 1948. Under this constitution, the executive branch, the legislative branch, and the judicial branch form the backbone of the administration. The president and prime minister, along with a cabinet called the Council of Ministers, make up the executive branch of the government. Members of the Council of Ministers are nominated by the prime minister and approved by the president. In Italy, the prime minister is called the President of the Council of Ministers.

The legislative branch of Italy's government creates bills, which may become law. Called *Parlamento*, or Parliament, this branch has two houses—the *Senato della Repubblica* or Senate and the *Camera dei Deputati* or Chamber of Deputies. Elected by popular vote, senators serve five-year terms. In addition to the 315 elected senators, the Senate includes a few lifelong members, such as Italy's former presidents. In the Chamber of

Deputies, 630 seats are filled by vote. These officials serve five-year terms. Officials in either house of Parliament may create legislative bills that need to be approved by both houses to become a law.

The third branch of government, the judicial branch, is the Constitutional Court (*Corte Costituzionale*). Italy's current judicial system is based in part on Roman law. Composed of fifteen judges, the court includes five judges appointed by the president, five elected by Parliament, and five elected by the ordinary and administrative supreme courts. Primarily, these judges make decisions on whether particular laws are constitutional.

National elections take place once every five years. Among Italian citizens, both men and women age eighteen and over may vote. The only exception is elections of senators. For these, minimum voting age is twenty-five.

For purposes of government and representation, Italy is divided into twenty regions (shown on most maps) and ninety-four provinces.

Italy has a number of political parties. Some of them are as follows: Forza Italia, Democratic Party of the Left, National Alliance, Northern League, United Christian Democrats, Democrats, Italian People's Party, Christian Democratic Center, Socialists, Communist-Renewal, Social Democratic, Republican, Liberal, Greens, and Italian Renewal.

Italy's government maintains friendly relations with the United States. Italy maintains an embassy in Washington, D.C. In 2002, Ferdinando Salleo served as the Italian ambassador to the United States. In addition, Italy has consulates in eight major cities: Boston, Chicago, Houston, Miami, New York, Los Angeles, Philadelphia, and San Francisco. Italy maintains similar friendly relations with other countries, such as Canada.

TIMELINE

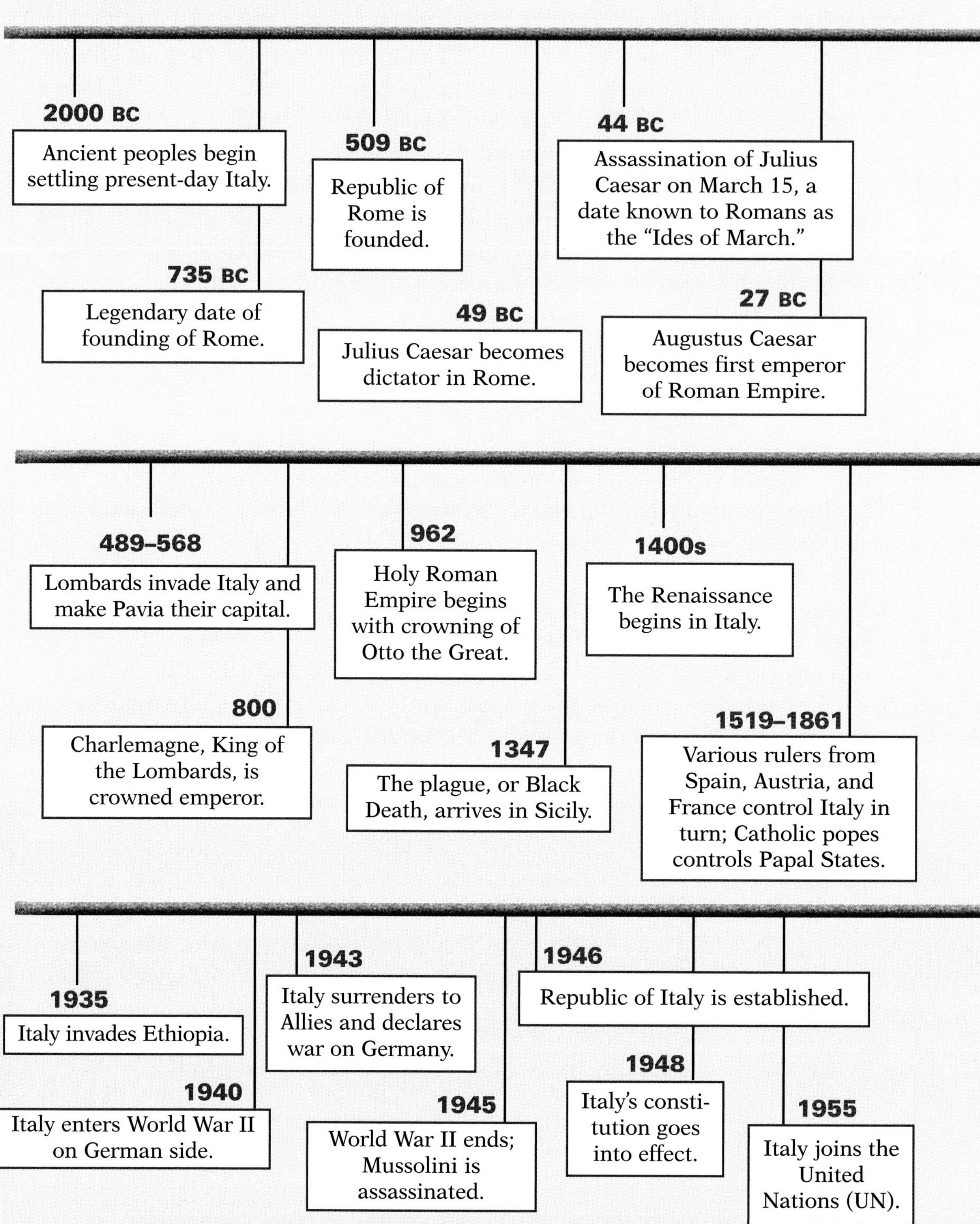

2000 BC
Ancient peoples begin settling present-day Italy.
735 BC
Legendary date of founding of Rome.
509 BC
Republic of Rome is founded.
49 BC
Julius Caesar becomes dictator in Rome.
44 BC
Assassination of Julius Caesar on March 15, a date known to Romans as the "Ides of March."
27 BC
Augustus Caesar becomes first emperor of Roman Empire.
489–568
Lombards invade Italy and make Pavia their capital.
800
Charlemagne, King of the Lombards, is crowned emperor.
962
Holy Roman Empire begins with crowning of Otto the Great.
1347
The plague, or Black Death, arrives in Sicily.
1400s
The Renaissance begins in Italy.
1519–1861
Various rulers from Spain, Austria, and France control Italy in turn; Catholic popes controls Papal States.
1935
Italy invades Ethiopia.
1940
Italy enters World War II on German side.
1943
Italy surrenders to Allies and declares war on Germany.
1945
World War II ends; Mussolini is assassinated.
1946
Republic of Italy is established.
1948
Italy's constitution goes into effect.
1955
Italy joins the United Nations (UN).

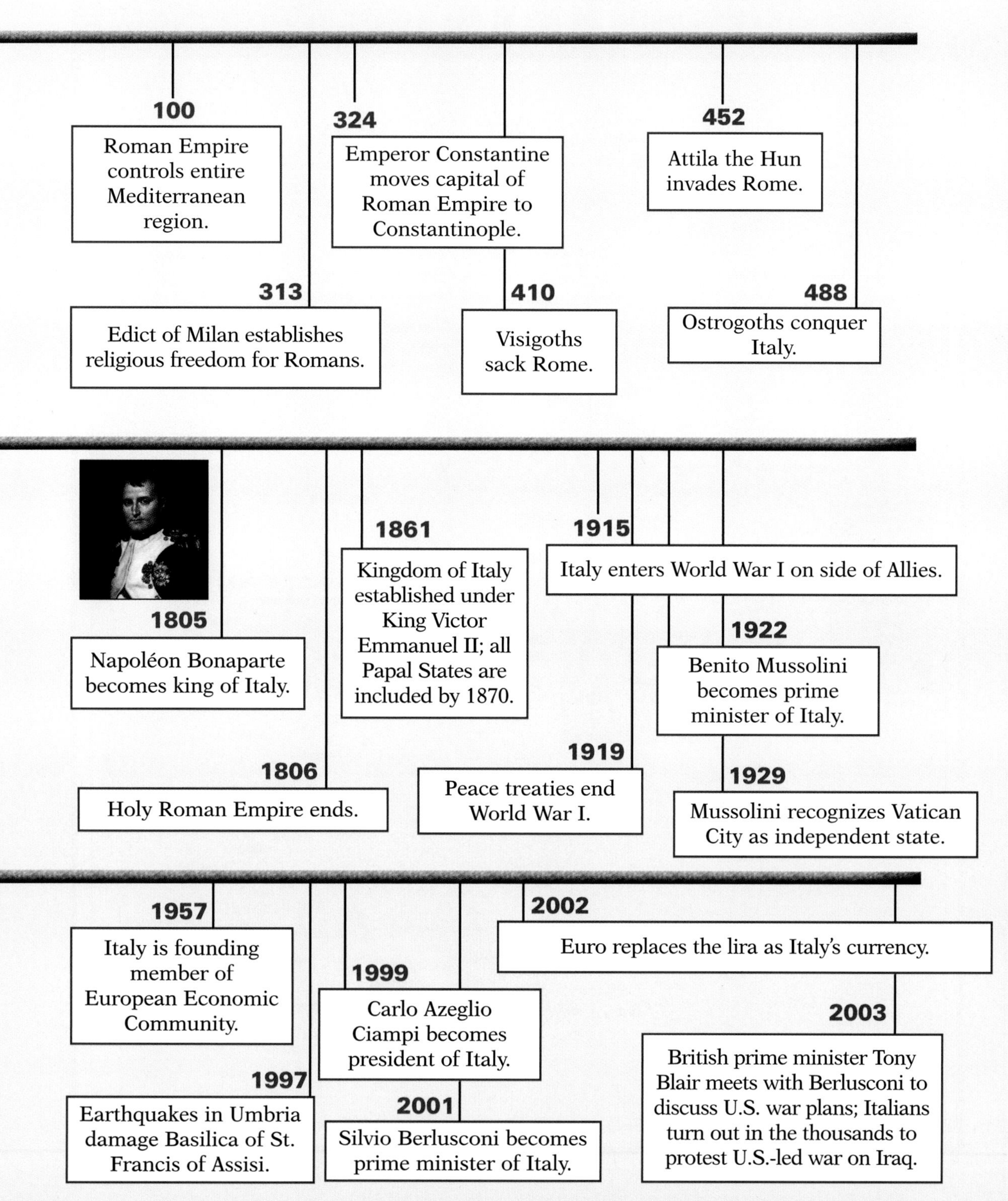
100
Roman Empire controls entire Mediterranean region.
313
Edict of Milan establishes religious freedom for Romans.
324
Emperor Constantine moves capital of Roman Empire to Constantinople.
410
Visigoths sack Rome.
452
Attila the Hun invades Rome.
488
Ostrogoths conquer Italy.
1805
Napoléon Bonaparte becomes king of Italy.
1806
Holy Roman Empire ends.
1861
Kingdom of Italy established under King Victor Emmanuel II; all Papal States are included by 1870.
1915
Italy enters World War I on side of Allies.
1919
Peace treaties end World War I.
1922
Benito Mussolini becomes prime minister of Italy.
1929
Mussolini recognizes Vatican City as independent state.
1957
Italy is founding member of European Economic Community.
1997
Earthquakes in Umbria damage Basilica of St. Francis of Assisi.
1999
Carlo Azeglio Ciampi becomes president of Italy.
2001
Silvio Berlusconi becomes prime minister of Italy.
2002
Euro replaces the lira as Italy's currency.
2003
British prime minister Tony Blair meets with Berlusconi to discuss U.S. war plans; Italians turn out in the thousands to protest U.S.-led war on Iraq.

ITALY

Legend
Ports/Harbors
Agriculture
Volcanoes
LIECHTENSTEIN
AUSTRIA
HUNGARY
SWITZERLAND
SLOVENIA
CROATIA
BOSNIA-H.
YUGOSLAVIA
FRANCE
S. Leonardo
Bolzano
Bormio
Madonna di Campiglio
Tarvisio
Tolmezzo
Spilimbergo
Trento
Sondrio
Domodossola
Verbania
San Pellegrino
Asiago
Pordenone
Udine
Latisana
Trieste
Aosta
Omegna
Varese
Bagolino
Treviso
Biella
Garda
Vicenza
Venice
Ceresole Reale
Novara
Ivrea
Milan
Brescia
Verona
Padova
Lodi
Mantova
Rovigo
Adria
GULF OF VENICE
Torino
Piacenza
Perosa Argentina
Asti
Parma
Canelli
Modena
Acceglio
Cuneo
Genoa
Bologna
Ravenna
Savona
Forlì
Firenzuola
Rimini
Albenga
La Spezia
Carrara
Pesaro
San Remo
GULF OF GENOA
Pisa
Florence
Ancona
LIGURIAN SEA
Cecina
Siena
Macerata
Montepulciano
Campiglia Marittimo
Assisi
ADRIATIC SEA
Grosseto
Todi
Spoleto
Corsica
FRANCE
Manciano
Viterbo
Pescara
L'Aquila
Chieti
Casalbordino
Montalto di Castro
Civitavecchia
The Vatican City
Avezzano
Palena
Casoli
Vieste
STRAIT OF OTRANTO
Fiuggi
Serracapriola
Manfredonia
Rome
Frosinone
Isernia
San Bartolomeo
Foggia
Trani
Bari
Latina
Sezze
Sabaudia
Gaeta
Cerignola
Monopoli
Caserta
Benevento
Castellana Grotte
Altamura
Naples
Avellino
Calitri
Rionero in Vulture
Brindisi
Castellammare
Salerno
Taranto
Lecce
Amalfi
Stigliano
Pisticci
Galatina
Sala Consilina
Sassari
Rotondella
Gallipoli
Camerota
Nuoro
Castrovillari
TYRRHENIAN SEA
Sardinia
Rossano
Belvedere Marittimo
Acri
Oristano
Cariati
Cirò Marina
Cosenza
Crotone
Amantea
Nicastro
Cagliari
Catanzaro
Tropea
Nicotera
Gioia Tauro
Cittanova
Sicily
IONIAN SEA
Siderno
Messina
Bovalino Marina
Palermo
MEDITERRANEAN SEA
Erice
Partinico
S. Fratello
Trapani
Bagheria
Cefalù
Bronte
Taormina
Alcamo
Gangi
Marsala
Troina
Partanna
Corleone
STRAIT OF SICILY
Enna
Catania
Mazara del Vallo
Ribera
Scordia
Sciacca
Riesi
Francofonte
Agrigento
Gela
Siracusa
Ragusa
Licata
Vittoria
Avola
ALGERIA
TUNISIA

ECONOMIC FACT SHEET

GDP in US$: $1.4 trillion

GDP Sectors: Agriculture 2.4%, industry 30%, services 67.6%

Land Use: Arable land 28%, permanent crops 10%, permanent pastures 15%, forests and woodland 23%, other 21%

Currency: 1 euro=100 euro cents. Notes: 5, 10, 20, 50, 100, 200, and 500 euro. Coins: 1, 2, 5, 10, 20, and 50 euro cents, 1 and 2 euro. U.S. $1=1.134 euro

Workforce: Services 63%, industry and commerce 32%, agriculture 5%

Major Agricultural Products: Wheat, rice, grapes, olives, citrus fruits

Major Exports: $243 billion—mechanical products, textiles, apparel, transportation equipment, metal products, chemical products, agricultural products

Major Imports: $226 billion—machinery and transport equipment, foodstuffs, ferrous and nonferrous metals, wool, cotton, energy products

Significant Trading Partners:

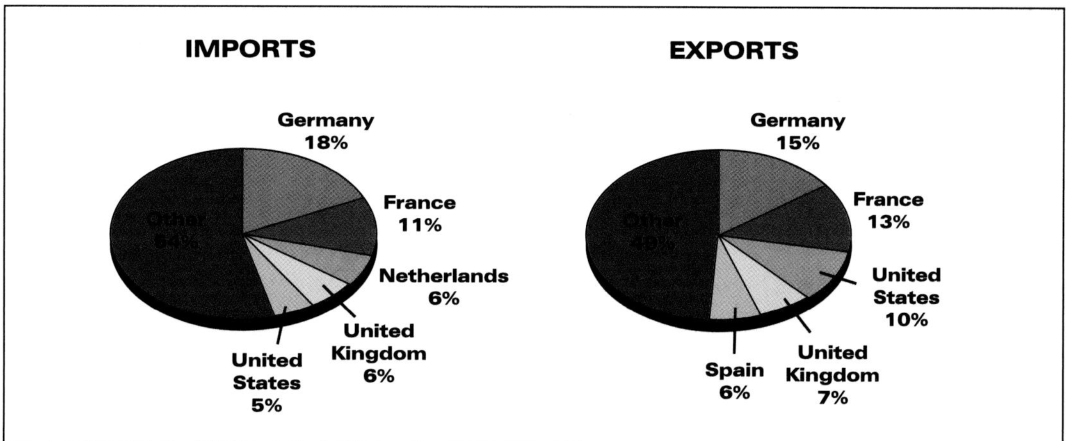

Rate of Unemployment: Approximately 10%

Highways: 417,918 miles (668,669 km)

Railroads: 12,366 miles (19,786 km)

Waterways: 1,500 miles (2,400 km)

Airports: 135

POLITICAL FACT SHEET

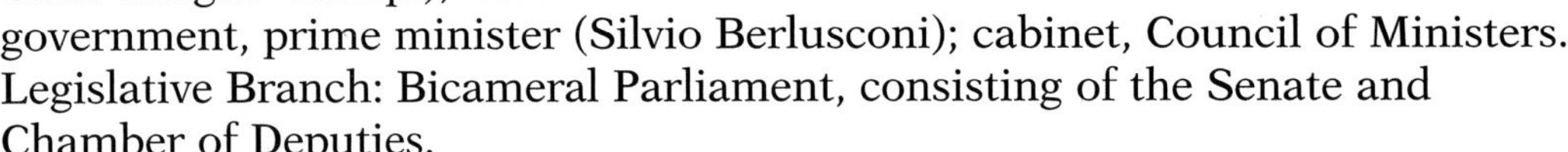

Official Country Name: *Repubblica Italiana* (Republic of Italy)

System of Government: Constitutional republic with two legislative houses.

Federal Structure: Executive Branch: chief of state, president Carlo Azeglio Ciampi); head of government, prime minister (Silvio Berlusconi); cabinet, Council of Ministers.
Legislative Branch: Bicameral Parliament, consisting of the Senate and Chamber of Deputies.
Judicial Branch: Constitutional Court, composed of fifteen judges.

Number of Registered Voters: 49,066,417 in 2000 (Eighteen years of age, universal, except in senatorial elections, where minimum age is twenty-five.)

National Anthem: "Fratelli d'Italia" ("Brothers of Italy")
Written by Goffredo Mameli, a poet who served in Italy's first War of Independence; Italy's national anthem was set to music by Michele Novaro in 1847. Known as "L'Inno di Mameli," it has been the country's anthem since 1946. Below is an excerpt:

Italian brothers,
Italy has arisen,
With Scipio's helmet
binding her head.
Where is Victory?
Let her bow down,
For God has made her
The slave of Rome.
Let us gather in legions,
Ready to die!
Italy has called!

CULTURAL FACT SHEET

Official Languages: Italian

Major Religion: Roman Catholicism

Capital: Rome

Population: 57.8 million

Ethnic Groups: Approximately 94% Italian, with small groups of German, French, Slovene-Italians in the north and Greek-and Albanian-Italians in the south

Life Expectancy: 79.25 years

Time: Greenwich Mean Time plus one hour (GMT+0100)

Literacy Rate: 98%

Cultural Leaders:

Visual Arts: Leonardo da Vinci (1452–1519), Michelangelo Buonarroti (1475–1564), Amedeo Modigliani (1884–1920), Giorgio de Chirico (1888–1978)

Literature: Dante Alighieri (1265–1321), Petrarch (1304–1374), Giovanni Boccaccio (1313–1375), Italo Calvino (1923–1985), Umberto Eco, (1932–)

Music: Giuseppe Verdi (1813–1901), Enrico Caruso (1873–1921), Luciano Pavarotti (1935–)

Entertainment and Sports: Roberto Rossellini (1906–1977), Rudolph Valentino (1895–1926), Sophia Loren (1934–), Luigi Pirandello (1867–1936), Alberto "La Bomba" Tomba (1966–), Bernardo Bertolucci (1940–)

National Holidays and Festivals:

New Year's Day: January 1
Epiphany: January 6
Easter Monday: March or April
Liberation Day: April 25
Labor Day: May 1
Republic Day: June 2
Assumption of the Virgin: August 15
All Saints' Day: November 1
National Unity Day: November 5
Immaculate Conception: December 8
Twelve Days of Christmas: December 25–January 5
St. Stephen's Day: December 26

GLOSSARY

Alpine (AL-PINE) Relating to the Alps, especially the highest area, above the timberline.

apostle (uh-PO-sel) One who is sent on a mission, especially that of carrying the message of the Christian religion.

artisan (ART-tee-zan) A skilled craftsperson.

deity (DEE-uh-tee) A figure of worship such as a god or goddess.

dictator (DIK-tay-ter) One who rules alone, with absolute power; dictators are often characterized as tyrants.

economy (ih-KAH-nuh-mee) A country's financial structure, including buying, selling, and inflation.

emperor (EM-per-er) One who rules an empire.

empire (EM-pyr) A vast political unit having many territories and a single ruler, usually an emperor or chief of state.

Fascism (FASH-ih-zum) A political movement characterized by tight control of society and the economy by the ruling power, suppression of opposition (for example, by banning political parties), and increased power of armed forces.

fertility (fur-TIL-it-tee) The state of being fruitful or productive.

fresco (FRES-koh) A colorful painting done on a plaster wall while the plaster is still wet.

glacier (GLAY-shur) A huge body of ice, usually one that moves slowly down a slope.

medieval (meh-DEE-vul) Time period of the Middle Ages, which is the period in European history between about AD 500 and 1500.

monarchy (MAH-nar-kee) A government that has a chief of state who rules for life; the monarch's powers may vary, from limited to absolute.

Papal State (PAY-pul STAYT) Territory in Italy ruled by the pope, from the eighth century to 1870.

peninsula (peh-NIN-suh-luh) A portion of land surrounded by water on three sides and connected to the mainland on the fourth side.

republic (ree-PUB-lik) A nation ruled by a chief of state and elected representatives, who govern according to established law.

tribunal (TRY-byoo-null) A court or forum of justice that decides public opinion.

FOR MORE INFORMATION

Embassy of Italy in Canada
275 Slater Street, 21st Floor
Ottawa, ON K1P 5H9
(613) 232-2401
Web site: http://www.italyincanada.com

Embassy of Italy in the United States
3000 Whitehaven Street NW
Washington, DC 20008
(202) 612-4400
Web site: http://www.italyemb.org

Italian Cultural Institute
425 Washington Street, Suite 200
San Francisco, CA 94111
(415) 788-7142
Web site: http://www.sfiic.org/

Web Sites

Due to the changing nature of Internet links, the Rosen Publishing Group, Inc., has developed an online list of Web sites related to the subject of this book. This site is updated regularly. Please use this link to access the list:

http://www.rosenlinks.com/pswc/ital

FOR FURTHER READING

Blashfield, Jean F. *Italy*. (Enchantment of the World, Second Series). New York: Children's Press, 1999.

Clare, John D, ed. *Italian Renaissance*. San Diego: Harcourt Brace, 1995.

Corbishley, Mike. *Everyday Life in Roman Times*. New York: Franklin Watts, 1994.

Hausam, Josephine Sander. *Italy*. Milwaukee, WI: Gareth Stevens Publishing, 1999.

Jovinelly, Joann. *The Crafts and Culture of the Romans*. New York: Rosen Publishing Group, 2002.

King, David C. *Italy: Gem of the Mediterranean*. New York: Benchmark Books, 1998.

Pickels, Dwayne E. *Roman Myths, Heroes, and Legends*. Philadelphia: Chelsea House Publishers, 1999.

BIBLIOGRAPHY

"Background Note: Italy." U.S. Department of State, Bureau of European and Eurasian Affairs. 2002. Retrieved May 6, 2002 (http://www.state.gov/r/pa/ei/bgn/4033pf.htm).

Clare, John D., ed. *Italian Renaissance*. San Diego: Harcourt Brace, 1995.

De'Medici, Lorenza, and Patrizia Passigli. *Italy: The Beautiful Cookbook: Authentic Recipes from the Regions of Italy*. San Francisco: HarperCollins Publishers, 1989.

Hale, John R. *Renaissance*. New York: Time-Life Books, 1965.

Hamilton, Edith. *Mythology*. Boston: Little, Brown and Co., 1942.

Holmes, George, ed. *The Oxford History of Italy*. New York: Oxford University Press, 1997.

"Italy." CIA, *The World Factbook* 2002. Retrieved October 27, 2002 (http://www.cia.gov/cia/publications/factbook/geos/it.html).

Norwich, John Julius, ed. *The Italians: History, Art, and the Genius of a People*. New York: Harry N. Abrams, 1983.

Travis, David. *The Land and People of Italy*. New York: HarperCollins, 1992.

PRIMARY SOURCE IMAGE LIST

Page 20: This sixth-century sarcophagus is now located at the Louvre Museum in Paris, France.
Page 21: This fourth-century mosaic depicts gladiators fighting.
Page 22 (top): An Etruscan gold coin that dates to the sixth century BC.
Page 22 (bottom): Dating from the nineteenth century, this illustration portrays Hannibal during the first Punic War.
Page 23: This engraving showing Rome, circa 1800, is now housed in the Stadtmuseum at Mantua, Italy.
Page 25: This second-century Roman mosaic is housed at the Musee Lapidaire in Vienne, France.
Page 26: This contemporary photograph shows the ruins of the Roman Forum in Rome, Italy.
Page 28 (top): This portrait of Cosimo de Medici by Agnolo Bronzino is located at the Uffizi Gallery in Florence, Italy.
Page 28 (bottom): This illustration of Marco Polo dates 1477 and is from the first edition of *Marco Polo's Travels*.
Page 29 (top): André Thevet drew this illustration of Amerigo Vespucci titled *Vrais Portraits et Vies de Hommes Illustres* in 1584.

Page 29 (bottom): This portrait, *Napoléon in His Study*, was painted in 1812 by Jacques-Louis David.
Page 30: A portrait of Victor Emmanuel II, circa 1865.
Page 31: An undated photograph of Giuseppe Garibaldi.
Page 32: A photograph of Benito Mussolini reviewing Italian boys who belonged to Fascist youth organizations.
Page 33 (top): This photograph of Mussolini in Genova appeared in the Italian magazine *Il Mattino Illustrato* on May 23, 1938.
Page 33 (bottom): This swastika pin depicting Hitler and Mussolini dates from 1936.
Page 34: A photograph taken by Thomas D. McAvoy shows a crowd gathered to hear Mussolini declare war in June 1940.
Page 35: The Italian Constitution in 1947 as it appeared in newspapers.
Page 36: A photograph of the members of the Italian Constituent Assembly approve the constitution of 1947.
Page 38: Aristotle's manuscript *Opera*, created by Girolamo da Cremona, is located in the Pierpont Morgan Library, New York.
Page 42: Gaius Plinius Secundus's (Pliny the Elder's) book *Historia Naturalis*, circa AD 77, is now housed in the Pierpont Morgan Library, New York.
Page 43: This Latin translation of Niccolò Machiavelli's book *Il Principe* was printed in 1513.
Page 44: This Etruscan red-figure bell crater from 360 BC is located in the Louvre Museum in Paris, France.
Page 45: Located in the atrium of the House of Vettii in Pompeii, this Roman mural dates circa AD 62.
Page 47: This first-century bronze of Jupiter is located in the Louvre Museum in Paris, France.
Page 48: This Roman mosaic of Orpheus from Dougga, Tunisia, is located at the Musee Archeologique in El Djem, Tunisia.
Page 50: Located at Capitoline Hill in Rome, the bronze statue *She-Wolf of the Capital* depicts twin brothers Romulus and Remus.
Page 51: A fresco titled *The Adoration of the King* was painted by Giotto di Bondone, circa 1305.
Page 52: This contemporary photograph shows the activity surrounding Carnevale festivities in Acireale, Sicily.
Page 57: Crowd in this present-day photograph watch the Italian Republican Guard's military horses at the Palio.
Page 58: This fresco *Saint Francis Preaching to the Animals* dates from the thirteenth century.
Page 63: Michelangelo finished painting the ceiling of the Sistine Chapel in Rome, Italy at the height of the Renaissance in 1512.
Page 64: A contemporary photograph of Saint Peter's Basilica.
Page 66: The *Ecstasy of Saint Francis*, created by Giotto di Bondone around 1300, is located in Assisi, Italy.
Page 67: Leonardo da Vinci's *The Last Supper*, painted around 1498, is displayed at the Santa Maria della Grazie in Milan, Italy.
Page 68: A contemporary photograph of the Shroud of Turin.
Page 69: This photograph of Padre Pio was taken in 1960.
Page 70: A contemporary photograph of the Trevi Fountain in Rome, Italy.
Page 71: A contemporary photograph of a Roman aqueduct in Sulmona, Italy.
Page 72: A contemporary photograph of the Roman Colosseum, in Rome, Italy.
Page 73: A contemporary photograph of the Leaning Tower of Pisa, located in Pisa, Italy.
Page 74: The dome of the Florence Cathedral was designed and built by Renaissance artist Filippo Brunelleschi in 1436.
Page 75 (top): *Mona Lisa*, by Leonardo da Vinci was painted around 1505 and is displayed in the Louvre Museum in Paris, France.
Page 75 (bottom): Michelangelo's statue *Pietà* was created around 1500 and is now housed in the Basilica di San Pietro in Rome, Italy.
Page 76: A fresco by Raphael Sanzio titled *The School of Athens* was painted around 1511 and is located in Rome, Italy.
Page 78: This contemporary photograph shows Florence's oldest surviving bridge, the Ponte Vecchio, constructed in 1345.
Page 79: This 2002 photograph of an auctioned Stradivarius violin was taken at Christie's Auction House in New York, New York.
Page 80: Located in the Bibliotheque Nationale in Paris, this fourteenth-century illustration by Giovanni Boccaccio is from *The Decameron*.

Primary Source Image List

Page 81: This undated portrait of Niccolò Machiavelli was painted by Santi di Tito.
Page 82: This photograph of Grazia Deledda was taken in 1927 by A. B. Lagrelius and Westphal.
Page 83: An engraving of Giosuè Carducci created by E. Mancastroppa after painting by Vittorio Corcos appeared in *L'Illustrazione* Italiana on July 17, 1892.
Page 84: This photograph of Luigi Pirandello appeared in 1919 in the Italian magazine *L'Illustrazione Italiana*.
Page 85: A color lithograph from the 1935 edition of Carlo Collodi's *Pinocchio* by Italian artist Atilio Mussino.
Page 86: This portrait of Antonio Stradivari at his workbench dates from 1690.
Page 87: This undated photograph shows Giacomo Puccini seated at a piano in Torre del Lago.
Page 88: An undated postcard shows a portrait of Giuseppe Verdi.
Page 105: A manuscript illustration titled *A Lecturer at the University of Bologna* dates from the fifteenth century.
Page 106: This portrait of Maria Montessori dates from 1920.
Page 112: This photograph of Ingrid Bergman and Roberto Rossellini was taken in Rome on October 30, 1951.

INDEX

About the Author: Lesli J. Favor's books include *Francisco Vázquez de Coronado: Famous Journeys to the American Southwest and Colonial New Mexico* and *Everything You Need to Know About Growth Spurts and Delayed Growth*. She has books coming out on Martin Van Buren and the Iroquois Confederacy. At the University of Texas at Arlington she earned her BA in English, then earned her MA and Ph.D. from the University of North Texas. Afterward, she was Assistant Professor of English at Sul Ross State University-Rio Grande College where she taught Children's Literature, among other courses. She lives in Dallas, Texas.

Designer: Geri Fletcher; **Cover Designer:** Tahara Hasan; **Editor:** Joann Jovinelly;
Photo Researcher: Gillian Harper; **Photo Research Assistant:** Fernanda Rocha